MW01259924

JESSIE COLE grew up in an isolated valley in northern New South Wales, where she still lives today in her childhood home. Her first novel, *Darkness on the Edge of Town*, was shortlisted for the 2013 ALS Gold Medal and longlisted for the Dobbie Literary Award. Her second novel, *Deeper Water*, was released in 2014 to critical acclaim.

Staying

Jessie Cole

A Memoir

TEXT PUBLISHING MELBOURNE AUSTRALIA

textpublishing.com.au

The Text Publishing Company
Swann House
22 William Street
Melbourne Victoria 3000
Australia

Copyright © Jessie Cole, 2018

The moral right of Jessie Cole to be identified as the author of this work has been asserted.

All rights reserved. Without limiting the rights under copyright above, no part of this publication shall be reproduced, stored in or introduced into a retrieval system, or transmitted in any form or by any means (electronic, mechanical, photocopying, recording or otherwise), without the prior permission of both the copyright owner and the publisher of this book.

Published by The Text Publishing Company, 2018

Cover design by W. H. Chong
Page design by Jessica Horrocks
Typeset by J&M Typesetting

Printed and bound in Australia by Griffin Press, an accredited ISO/NZS 14001:2004 Environmental Management System printer

ISBN: 9781925603507 (paperback)
ISBN: 9781925626544 (ebook)

A catalogue record for this book is available from the National Library of Australia

This book is printed on paper certified against the Forest Stewardship Council® Standards. Griffin Press holds FSC chain-of-custody certification SGS-COC-005088. FSC promotes environmentally responsible, socially beneficial and economically viable management of the world's forests.

This project has been assisted by the Australian Government through the Australia Council, its arts funding and advisory body.

For all those left behind

Contents

●

Threshold

The car hums. It is parked in the garage. The forest ticks around it—the cracking of branches, the buzz of crickets, the light swish of leaves as they fall down from the trees. The spiders scuttle about repairing their webs. A possum shrieks off in the distance. The stray ginger cat haunts the periphery.

But inside the car my father is breathless.

In a few hours my mother will find him. He won't answer his phone and she will know, and she will drive out from the yellow beach shack to check. She will find him, dead, and go inside and call the ambulance and our friends from down the road. Then she will wait with my father, listening to the sounds of the forest. Our friends will arrive first, because they aren't far away, and they will clean the blood from the bathroom, from where my father tried to slit his wrists, so my mother doesn't have to. The police and ambulance will come, and they will take his body away. Later, we will receive an ambulance bill, addressed to my father, though he was dead when the paramedics arrived and they could not revive him. His name on that envelope will hit us like a punch to the solar plexus.

But let's go back. To the humming car in the garage. To my father's last thoughts.

He is lying across the back seat, his eyes closed, blocking out the world. The pressure of his tortured grief is slowly lessening in his chest. There is the faintest hint of relief. But he knows that he has failed us, and that must weigh upon him too. Scratched out beside him lies a note.

Billie, Jessie, Jakey—I'm sorry. Janny—I love you.

And it is all there, in those words. The life we had and the life we lost.

Home

Since my father's suicide, the word 'trust' has gotten under my skin. If someone should utter it as a way to soothe me, I will go someplace quiet and cry. The very word has become broken. I hear in it only the echoes of its opposite. Hints of leavings, endings, goodbyes. Whispers of risk, hurt, harm. But it was not this way from the outset. I was born four weeks early— a premmie baby—delicate and clingy like a nursling possum. My mother tells me I barely slept. She says that in the middle of the night my father brought me up onto his chest, his strong heart-beat banging there beneath my tiny ear. And I would slip straight into sleep, because there was no safer place.

≈

My earliest memories all involve the nourishment I found in my parents' bodies. A feeling of being held, of skin settling against skin. I remember no tussles over privacy or space, more a surrender of their bodies to mine. *You are welcome here*, their touch seemed to say. *Come, make yourself at home.* I slept between them, rolling from one pair of arms to the next. They each had their own smell, distinct and animal. My father had a tiny thatch of hair in the middle of his chest, no more than twenty strands, and pressed up against him in the early mornings I petted it like a pelt. My mother let me play a game, a womb-game, though I didn't call it that. She curled up on her side and I snuggled into the triangle between her knees and chest. 'Cubbies,' I murmured, 'let's play cubbies,' and she never refused. My brother was born when I was twenty months old. My parents' friends, who lived next door, came over to babysit me while my mother gave birth, and I woke in the night to their unfamiliar bodies. The woman whispered, 'Mummy will be home soon, Mummy will be home soon,' and I could feel the anxiety seeping out around her. She seemed concerned I might not believe her, but there was nothing I was more certain of.

≈

I was born in the late 1970s, when—in northern New South Wales at least—everything was up for grabs. Right and wrong were social constructs, conventionality was spurned, conformity worth escaping and money-making passé. Polyamory was the new frontier. Drugs and alcohol, dreaming and philosophy. Anything could happen and probably did.

In among this jumble of living experiments, my parents decided to test the hypothesis that children were born pure—that the less you interfered with their natural goodness, the less damage you did. They were not the first to propose such a radical theory. D. H. Lawrence once set out three rules of childcare: *How to begin to educate a child. First rule, leave him alone. Second rule, leave him alone. Third rule, leave him alone. That is the whole beginning.* My parents did little to actively socialise us. I can only assume they believed my brother, Jake, and I would learn by example. We watched my mother's brow carefully for signs of displeasure, and it was a fairly reliable indicator, but there were few rules and few explanations. We weren't required to use words like 'please' or 'thank you'. Clothes were optional. We ate all our food with spoons. We didn't have a bedtime. Sometimes when we were rowdy or wild our father would yell, and we'd stand by, quietly ashamed, but our mother would swoop down and say, 'Oh, they're not naughty—they're just tired.' And we would smile, all our goodness restored.

We lived far outside of town, nestled in green hills, on a winding dead-end road in a tiny town called Burringbar. Filled with hopes for a new start, a tree-change—another world—my parents had packed up their busy Sydney lives for the freedom of the country. They had bought a few acres of pasture and set about planting out a magnificent garden. A forest. When I was little the trees were little too, saplings, and we all grew together, from nothing much to something. Maybe all children believe their parents create the world, but in my case it appeared to be true. In the first year my parents lived at Burringbar they oversaw the building of a house. It was experimental too, all its rooms separated by the quick-growing forest. Our home sprang up around me, as the garden had before it, my parents' vision becoming quickly manifest.

Running down the centre was a long, open walkway paved with bricks. From the edges of the walkway the rooms spread like islands. The garden was the deep green sea, the bedrooms private cloistered worlds. The walkway led to a highset pavilion with a sloping wooden-shingled roof. Temple-like, it presided over the house. Palms and bromeliads grew thick between the rooms, and through the large sliding glass doors all that could be seen was a multitude of dense greens with an occasional stripe of colour, a bromeliad in flower. Walking through the doors into the garden there was no drop, no step—it was just a slow, indefinite drift outside.

Back then, the world seemed a welcoming place. The bush-land surrounding us was full of creatures: lizards, birds, snakes, frogs, toads, ants, beetles, bees. We had a dog and two cats and a pet magpie, Georgie, who with a little coaxing would perch on my mother's arm. Once a giant goanna came out from the forest and plodded, dinosaur-like, down the open walkway. We stood to watch it, letting it pass. Eventually it scurried under a cush-ioned bench. 'I'll get it!' I cried, clambering beneath the bench, hands outstretched. The goanna scratched me, bloody lines all up my arms. I screamed in outrage, my panicking mother wrenching me out by my feet. I was bewildered—why didn't it want to play?

I once caught a bush-mouse with my bare hands. In that moment I loved it fiercely, its little grey body trembling in my palms, but it bit me, hard, until I let it go. I collected ants, gently pinching them between my tiny fingertips—even the big biting ones. I manhandled the skinks, the frogs, the beetles. A snail was an exciting find, since we didn't really have them. I even enjoyed the leeches, the way they wanted to hang around. Everything seemed right in the world—and if I loved these creatures, why wouldn't they love me back? That, I believe, was my thinking. Even so, it was hard to get the captured bush-mouse to give me much affection.

≈

My father was a psychiatrist, but he only worked three days a week. On his days off he toiled in the garden. He began fantastical tasks and finished them in a single day. Covered in sweat and dirt, with an aching back and a tired body, he came in and told my mother of his progress. A Japanese garden, with a real slated pond and giant boulders and bamboo. An orchard with rows of citrus that buzzed merrily with bees. A rainforest, shady and ancient-seeming, strewn with fallen coloured leaves.

Coming in one night, dirt-speckled and sour-smelling, my father showed us a vividly white ball, smaller than one of our marbles. Jake and I sat steaming in the bath, naked and easy, the leaves of the growing forest outside whispering wordless secrets in our ears. The bathroom rested among the trees, the sliding glass doors open to the green.

With a delicate tug he pulled this small sphere apart

and thousands of tiny spiders fell, sprinkling down upon us. Minuscule, they spread across the water, floating towards the edges, their legs braced against the sway of our careful movements. Hurriedly, the masses of baby spiders climbed out and along the top of the old enamel bathtub. With concentrated joy, we scooped out the stragglers and flicked them gently from our fingers and out the open doorway into the forest. I stared in wonder that so many had come from such a small, seamless pouch. Where would they all go when they were grown?

I understood that my father had held the power of their lives—and deaths—within his gentle hands, and felt in a subtle way that he had created them. I searched his face for signs of meaning, but he was unreadable and unexpectedly quiet. My mother came in from the kitchen to see what had caused our squeals, and I checked to see how deep the crease between her brows became when she saw the tiny wafting spiders.

'They're not biting ones, Mum.'

My mother's face broke into a smile.

'They're amazing.' Her words were soft. 'Where did you find them?'

He motioned out towards the garden, and my parents wandered off together in search of the very spot.

≈

When my father was at work, my mother took us down to the waterhole. Right at the edge there was a rock—a boulder—with dips and curves that fit my mother's naked body precisely. We called the boulder 'the rock', but in my head it was *my mother's rock*. I believed the rock had been shaped by her, that those dips and hollows were a tangible response to who my mother was.

We spent whole days down at the waterhole, my mother settling into the curves of her rock, drinking up the sun. Sometimes she let us inspect her. We examined her breasts, lifted her arms to look at her armpits, opened her legs to peer into the place we knew we'd come from. My mother sighed, not exasperated, just, perhaps, resigned. She'd say, 'You can look, but don't touch,' and we would look and look and look.

Besides my mother's body, there were many things of interest at the waterhole: eels, catfish, turtles, guppies, waterspiders, tadpoles, frogs, ducks, speedy-bugs, ochre painting-rocks, skimming-rocks, the occasional spot of clay or the much sought-after growth of soft, floating luminescent slime. Hours would pass where we barely looked up, the world around us so utterly absorbing.

Years later, when I had children of my own, I lay down on my mother's rock, believing I'd have grown into the hollows and dips, thinking that maybe now it was *my* rock, but it never did fit my curves. All my childhood I assumed it to be the most comfortable place, if only I was big enough to fit it. A mould—shaped by my mother—that I would one day grow into, but I never did.

≈

Some things were solid, unchanging. The sun rose in the sky, it was colder by night than by day, the ants swarmed inside the house before it rained—but very little was truly the same from day to day.

Swimming in the creek that surrounded our home, I was aware of every rock beneath my feet—the particularity of its placement—and where to rest my soles below the shadowy surface of the water. Everything was familiar, every random fern, every small palm, but daily new things would arise. Any number of seeds falling from above, inexplicable sudden leaf drops, branches cleaving from trees, holes dug in the banks by unseen mysterious animals, the sudden booming whoosh of flock pigeons taking off into the sky. The smallest of shifts and the land was new.

Most years the creeks flooded and everything shifted. Giant deposits of stones filled in sections that were once deep. Streams snaked sideways, taking different paths. Enormous tree trunks arrived from upstream where once there had been none. The whole world had to be relearned from scratch, and with each flood it all happened again and again. A paradoxical knowledge slowly grew inside me: things were unchanging but simultaneously in flux. And with this knowledge, the subtle awareness that I was part of the process. The house and garden—the land—an extension of me, or I an extension of it? Growing and changing, evolving, like one giant organism. As the years went by, the garden, the natural world, began slowly taking over the house. I was—we all were—just inhabitants in this moving symphony of nature, part of the ecosystem at large.

Growing up, the connectedness I felt to my homeplace was as intrinsic to my sense of self as my connectedness to family. In fact, it felt very similar. I believed all the animals around me were kin, as many children do, but it was more than that. I sensed a sort of receptivity from the plants, from the water, from the soil. Wind and storms were life forces—even the rain had character. The garden itself reached out and caressed me as I passed. Nature wasn't static or non-involved; it was present, tender. As children, Jake and I didn't pick the flowers, because they belonged with the trees. We loved them, with their bright, beaming faces, and they seemed to love us in return.

≈

In life, my father was tallish but not too tall. He was generally dark of feature: dark-eyed, dark-haired, darkish skin, big bushy dark brows. Looking at photos, I can see he had been quite handsome as a young man, though I never thought of him that way. He was corporal, flesh and blood, and I experienced him largely through touch.

On the weekends my parents got up early and drove us to the beach. My father's smile was wide as he faced the waves. When I ran to him, he scooped me up with one hand as though I weighed nothing. He loved the sea, and I loved it too.

'Take me out, Dad—take me out past the waves.'

'You want to go all the way out there?' His voice was serious, but his eyes were light and shining.

'Yeah, with you.'

'Okay, but we'll have to go under them.'

Holding me, he waved to my mother and Jake, motioning with his spare hand that he was going out. We ignored the subtle crease of my mother's brow.

My father strode at first, the waves surging against his legs and crashing about my feet, and when the water reached his waist he nodded that it was time to go under.

The waves were roaring and white, deep and swelling.

Salt and sand.

Surfacing, we spluttered and shook our heads and I wiped my tangled, matted hair from my eyes.

'Dumpers,' he whispered, close to my ear.

I clung on strongly, and when the next wave came my father dived beneath it. We could feel its power churning above us and we stayed down deep until I thought my chest would burst. Each wave was bigger than the next, until getting out to the open water was a serious business, and then finally we were clear. The green expanse of ocean lay before us. I swam about, my father floating there beside me, and when I was tired I slung my arms around his neck to rest. My father smelled of salt, and I snuffled my nose against his prickly jaw and touched a trickle of water on his throat with my tongue.

≈

When I was a child my father drew pictures that he always signed with a mandala. A circle with an 'x' inside. I never asked him what the mandala meant, though he seemed to use it as a kind of symbol for himself. In many ways these drawings were more like diaries. A remarkable number of them were about fathering. Portraits of us kids, mixed in with poems and musings. Sometimes he would let me help him. He'd give over a section of the paper for me to colour with oil pastels while he sketched. The drawings were important to him. He had each one professionally framed, and they hung, scattered about, on all our walls. Visual representations, sometimes alarming, of what was in his head. As a young man, he'd wanted to be an artist, but—pressured by his father—he'd trained as a doctor instead. Psychiatry, where he'd ended up, seemed a specialty well suited to his embracing of the unusual.

≈

My brother and I had our own language, a kind of unspoken exchange filled with intricate nuance. Born not quite two years apart, we fitted together like the intertwined fingers of clasping hands, and then, dovetailed, grew in opposite directions. I was all authority and plans, urgent, and brimming with bubbling words. Quiet and watchful, Jake was tirelessly gentle. Our play was a simple arrangement: I provided the structure—*the game*— and Jake filled in all the missing parts. My brother spoke very little, but he chose his words well. Silence crept about him like a low mist. Jake stepped back from the world, but he didn't step back from me. Sure and unflinching, I told my brother where I wanted him to be, and why, and he stayed close, holding my gaze to check that all was still right. Peering into my brother's face, I saw the questions he asked. I heard his voice in my head, though he only said a word here and there. I listened to the sound of his gaze and I answered him in speech.

In those days we had a parade of visitors. My parents' old city friends who'd come to stay, or new neighbours who'd drop around unannounced. Shy and sweet, with bottomless brown eyes, Jake was loved by every passing adult. But when a stranger broke into our imaginary world, he backed away in fright.

'What are you kids playing?' someone would ask.

Stepping forward, I'd explain our game, chatting and bouncing about, distracting them from my brother's startled face.

'So, Jakey, what have *you* been doing?' the intruder would say.

Jake looked down at the ground, but in small moments of bravery he glanced up at me, his eyes imploring, and I knew to try to rescue him.

'Jake's been playing with me, and yesterday we went to the beach, but he didn't swim out past the waves like me. He likes the little waves and the shells that look like open mouths. Jake loves those pipi ones.'

The eyes of the intruder slid from me to Jake. 'I asked *Jake* what he's been doing, Jess. You shouldn't talk over your brother.'

I'd step aside then, all my bounce gone. Jake would peek at me from behind the intruder. I could see he felt pinned to the wall. My brother whispered a few stray words and the adult would move on. Stepping back within the circle of our own private world, my brother and I were silent, our certainty ruffled. We stood a minute, deflated, until finally we fell upon the next game and raced off, united and forgetting.

Standing between Jake and the world, I was an interpreter for my delicate-hearted brother. Jake was my shadow, and I his voice. Probably I was smothering sometimes, but unlike the little bush-mouse, my brother never did bite.

≈

Most of us are born into a family, however flimsy or strong. We form narratives of who we are, stringing our memories into stories, forever working to create meaning, a story arc of sorts. But memories are as slippery as fish, darting off, unreachable, or surrounding us in shoals, circling thick and fast. It's easy to assume that families have a shared narrative—a basic truth we all agree on—but every person stands in their own particular place in history. Haunted, damaged or unhindered to varying degrees.

When my parents moved from Sydney to northern New South Wales, they left behind my father's daughters from his previous marriage. Billie and Zoe, eight and six, stayed with their mother, though they visited in the school holidays. These older sisters were born into a different family from the one I came to inhabit. I entered the world unaware that my father had tried this before. That when his first attempt fell apart, he'd tried it again. From the place where I began, in the middle of this melded family, I struggled to catch up with all the parts I had missed. My sisters' lives without me—mysterious, beguiling.

≈

Every school holidays my sisters flew up to Burringbar to visit. Quite often they would miss their flight. Waiting for their arrival at the other end, I imagined the rush to get to the airport, their mother yelling as they ran for the car, each one dragging bags behind her. The inevitable traffic jam on the way there. The madcap race through the terminal to the check-in counter, then the slump of their mother's shoulders when the man at the desk told them they were too late. In my imaginings, their mother turned to them, their bags bursting at the seams with last-minute additions, and said simply, 'Let's ring your dad.'

Straightening her shoulders, their mother walked off. She found a payphone, scrambled in her handbag until she found some change, and without hesitation made the call.

They had missed the plane—again.

And then the wait. The horrible wait on stand-by for the next flight. Their mother trying not to be cross because she had planned her day and now she was stuck waiting in the dirty airport with not enough money for lunch, and maybe there would be no space for them on the next plane anyway.

But there was.

And when my sisters arrived, we were waiting, sunburned

and wave-tossed. Me and Jake—the little ones—hardly more than babies. By missing the plane my sisters had missed the beach, and they scanned our bodies, taking in the sand still sprinkled across our feet. We all stood a moment while our father collected up the bags and put them on a trolley. Billie yawned, looking out towards the car park. Zoe watched as I hid behind my mother's legs, then ducked out and lifted my dress to show her my new frilly underpants. She laughed, but when Jake—who was two and a half already—put his hand down the front of my mother's shirt to feel for her breast, Zoe looked across at Billie and I could tell they were embarrassed.

'Isn't he too old for that?' Zoe asked.

'He's just a baby.' My mother's voice was mild. She smoothed Jake's wispy hair and leaned forward to kiss the top of his head. 'What do you think? Has he gotten big?'

'Does he still poo in a nappy?'

My mother laughed, and I climbed up onto the trolley with the bags, squashing them and giggling.

'We ready?' our father called, his gaze shifting from his half-grown daughters, searching out my mother's eyes. She nodded, absently kissing my brother's head one last time, and we all turned to walk towards the car.

We were grouped in twos, these sibling sets. The big girls and the little ones. I tended to think of my big sisters as a homogeneous duo, when of course they were very singular people. Billie: tall from early on, sensible, contained, frighteningly articulate, precociously intelligent. Zoe: vibrant, impulsive, expressive, pretty in a way that never went unnoticed. I was fascinated by them both, but I watched Zoe more. She was unpredictable— I never knew what she might do.

Back home—after the stifling heat of the car—my sisters raced to put on their swimmers and skipped down the uneven steps to the waterhole. My mother followed, her pace slow and careful with us little ones in tow. Our father scooped me up as he passed, carrying me to the bottom. My sisters jumped nimbly from rock to rock across the rapids to the darker water of the round pool. They had come to Burringbar often enough to be fearless of the deep unknown of the water, and without pause they plunged in, laughing.

'Throw me a board, Dad,' Billie called. 'I just want to float.'

Still carrying me, my father tossed a boogie board across the water. Billie lay on the board, belly down, her face to the side, eyes closed, the water lapping at her cheek. I watched her from my perch on my father's hip, wondering what she was thinking.

Zoe swept underneath the water, her body sleek. Resurfacing, she looked across at us, our father and me.

'Do you want to go in, Pygmy?' he asked me.

Ignoring him, I wriggled free of his arms. 'You're a good swimmer, Zoe!' I called. Jake and I were always naked, and I stared at Zoe's bikini. 'I can swim too!'

'Show me, then.'

Zoe watched as I entered the water and proudly paddled about. She smiled across at me, and then looked up at our dad. 'Why do you call her Pygmy?'

'Pygmy Fats.'

'Pygmy Fats?'

'She's like a little pygmy with a big round tummy—aren't you, Jess?'

Scrambling out of the water, I stood on the bank, pushing my stomach out as far as it would go. 'It's big. It's bigger than Jake's.'

Zoe turned away and plunged back under the water. Swimming out past Billie still floating on the board, she clambered up onto the grassy bank on the other side of the waterhole. Our father dived in after her, his body making a whacking sound as it hit the water. I wandered up the sloping bank and plunked down into my mother's lap. Sliding against her body, I nestled in beside Jake, who suckled distractedly at her breast, and my brother reached out a hand to swipe at my scraggly hair. I watched the girls and our father in the water.

Our father swam to where Zoe was crouched on the bank, his body long and straight across the water, only the top of his head peeking out. When he neared, he slowly lifted his eyes and then his mouth and growled in a deep, low voice, 'The crocodile is coming to get you …'

Zoe smiled then, her lively big-toothed grin.

'I'm not scared of the crocodile!' She launched herself onto our father's back and he went under with the weight of her. Resurfacing, he pulled Zoe off, and with a tussle pushed her under the water. She came up spluttering and laughing and he wrapped his arm around her in a dripping, easy embrace.

'I've missed you girls,' he said, squeezing her shoulder. 'What's been going on?'

'Nothing.' Zoe jerked out from beneath his arm. 'Dad, why don't you ever call?'

Billie raised her head, looking across at the two of them. She touched her feet to the bottom, letting the board go. Zoe's question hung there in the air.

Our father didn't answer, lying flat instead. 'The crocodile is coming to get you …'

'Come on, Dad—we're too old for that game,' Billie called from across the creek.

I jumped up from my mother's lap and raced down the bank. 'I'm not scared of the crocodile, Daddy! Come and get me!'

Stretching out along the water, our father glided towards me. He eyed me ominously from the shallows and I slipped a toe into the water. He waited till I stood with both legs in the creek, then reached up a hand and grabbed me. Squealing as he pulled me out into the water, I thrashed about trying to escape him, but in a minute I gave up and hung my arms about his neck. With a nudge he slid me onto his back.

Standing on the bank, her arms limp at her sides, Zoe watched as we floated together around the creek. I glanced across at Billie, but she was floating again on the boogie board, not paying us any heed.

'You tired, Zoe?' I heard my mother ask. 'You want to go up? Come on.'

Detaching Jake from her breast, my mother set him on the

ground. My brother smiled at Zoe, a sudden, open, goofy grin, as though he'd only just realised that he knew who she was.

Jake reached out a hand towards her.

'He's got something for you,' my mother said.

Zoe took the rich blood-red leaf Jake held in his hand, and he smiled again—his sweet, dark-eyed smile.

'It's beautiful. Thanks, Jakey.'

'It's a quondong leaf,' my mother explained. 'They're lovely, aren't they?' She tousled Zoe's cropped hair. 'Are you hungry? I'll make you a sandwich when we get up.'

My mother called to me to come up too, but I clung to my father's shoulders and shook my head.

'She can stay down a bit longer, Janny. She's with me.'

As a little girl, it was hard for me to conceive that my relationship with my father might be difficult for my sisters. I could only understand their connection to him from what I myself had experienced: the ease, the confidence, the love, the trust. It is always tricky to stand in another's shoes, and perhaps as a child it is even harder. I didn't see that I was flaunting an intimacy my sisters found painful, though in hindsight it is all there, in plain view.

≈

I never visited any of the houses Billie and Zoe lived in with their mother. I knew almost nothing concrete about their other life, but I collected all the details I could scrounge: their mother's new marriages, all the times they moved, the names of their pet goats, the uneasy sibling rivalry between them, and all the wrangling with their assorted exotic-sounding schoolfriends. I was endlessly curious about this world my sisters flew in from and flew back to. Billie and Zoe brought with them a kind of glamour, a cool. They wore different clothes, had different belongings and knew slang words we'd never heard. But it was their attitude to us—an aloof detachment—that made them most alluring. Billie, eight years older than me and generally in charge, didn't even bother bossing Jake and me around, we were that unimportant, whereas Zoe usually set me some kind of test.

'Here, Jess, I'll draw a picture and we'll see how much better you can colour inside the lines.' I still remember the exact outline of the little girl she drew. 'Let's see how grown-up you are.'

I was attentive, wanting to show progress. I started off carefully, but closer to the end I got tired and my texta slipped.

'That's pretty good,' Zoe conceded. 'Still a bit messy in this part, though.'

When my sisters visited they always fought over who got to sit next to my brother, and the loser was stuck with me. I didn't understand why I was so second-rate, though I loved my brother as much as they did. Jake didn't have to try to be kind—he just was. I was resigned to my sisters' favouritism, but it still stung. When the big girls came to stay I went from being the oldest child, with all the accompanying advantages, to the third child, disempowered and overlooked.

Unlike Jake and me, the big girls had been trained by their

mother in manners and propriety. They knew how to use a knife and fork. They thought us barbarians—of course—with our unbrushed hair and dirty fingernails. Sometimes my parents would leave my sisters in charge and head off somewhere for lunch. Billie and Zoe, forced to take an interest, took these opportunities to give us lessons in all the things we'd missed. They set the table, elaborately, and then made us sit down and eat. We thought it a game. They prowled around us, rulers in hand to whack us with when we made mistakes. No elbows on the table. No knees up. Chewing with your mouth closed. Fork in left hand, knife in right. It was fun at first, but after a few whacks it seemed a punishment. And what was wrong with elbows on the table anyway?

I was always excited about school holidays when my sisters came to visit, but deep down I was also relieved to see them go. They had high standards, and I felt myself always judged wanting.

≈

At home, the 1970s morphed into the 1980s. It was a time of fresh starts. My parents believed they could leave the past behind, that they could sculpt a world they wanted to live in, freed from the shackles of extended family or outdated rules. And in many ways they did. We barely saw our grandparents, aunts or uncles—they were very distant figures—but my parents had frequent extended Sunday lunches with old friends and new. Car wheels scraped against the white pebbles of the driveway, signalling arrival, and Jake and I ran out the front to greet the guests. Wandering down the walkway, bottles of wine in hand, the adults went straight up to the pavilion while we sped off towards the garden.

Many of my parents' friends had children around my age. In those days we all seemed part of a chaotic kind of family. I had real cousins, out in the world, who I never saw, though I had memorised their names—but these other children felt cousin-like. Sometimes even sibling-ish.

'See the cubbyhouse me and Jake made?'

A haphazard structure built of chairs, an overturned table and several umbrellas all covered in multicoloured rugs sagged slightly sideways in the front garden like a tropical igloo.

'Did your mum let you use the good blankets?' one of the kids piped up.

'She always does,' I chirped. 'We don't even have to put them back!'

The boundaries between us were blurry.

'Let's go into our room and play,' someone would say, pointing to the island bedroom my brother and I shared. Our toys were theirs and theirs were ours. There was a collectiveness to everything.

Ours.

At these lunches, my mother cooked in the kitchen, bringing steaming saucepans full of spicy-smelling curries up to the pavilion, while Jake and I ran about with these other wild children. Playing and fighting, screaming and laughing, we were left to our own devices—but hourly, with raucous voices raised in a communal singsong chant, we approached the adults as they lounged in the pavilion.

'We want to go down the creek! Are you ready yet?'

'Not yet. Soon.'

After eating and drinking their fill, and chatting for hours, the adults wandered about the garden together, tipsy and hot, to view the paradise being sculpted by my father's hands.

Then, finally, they began the descent to the waterhole.

The whole party trooped down the forest steps and picked their way awkwardly across the rapids. Standing on the bank, milling about, the adults laughed while all the children stripped off and jumped in. My mother, who drank little, was on patrol, and she sat on the rock and silently counted heads. The children leaped and cavorted, squealed and splashed, and called and called for their parents to watch them.

'Watch me stand on the boogie board, Mum!' Jake's legs wobbled as he balanced on the board.

'I can swim under the water for twenty seconds, Dad!'

'Watch me! Watch me! Watch me!'

My mother watched and watched while the adults' uproarious laughter rang out across the water. Sometimes the men got in and played—tossing and yelling and dunking—and when everyone was cool again we all crossed the sliding rapids and tramped, dripping, back up the hill to rest awhile after the breathless pleasure of the water. The visitors, sobered by the freshness of the waterhole, drifted back to their own green worlds tucked away in the surrounding hills.

And then there were the parties, the slow glide into night while the house filled to bursting. People seeping out the open doorways and into the garden sea, unconcerned by the darkness lapping at their feet. Sometimes my father hired a band, setting them up in the pavilion, and the adults danced and danced until the place shook with stomping feet. Everyone brought a plate and there was endless food and a bathtub filled with alcohol and ice. Jake and I snuck in with our co-conspirators and stole ice from the bathroom to suck between our teeth. Together with the other kids we traversed the terrain of the party, a labyrinth of infinite paths. Crawling beneath the action, we weaved between the unsteady legs of our parents, spilling into the blackness of the night, brimming with infectious giggles. We took torches into the garden and played games outside, the torchlight making tunnels of brightness in this otherwise dark world. Playing and playing, until, finally exhausted, we curled up in some hideaway and fell asleep. Late in the night, the mothers searched for us and found us sleeping in our rumpled party clothes. Bundling us up, dirty and dishevelled, they slid us into bed.

≈

I was seven when Zoe came to live in Burringbar, and she was thirteen. Billie stayed behind. No explanation was offered for this change in living arrangements, though—through judicious eavesdropping—I had gathered it was something to do with a clash between Zoe and her mother's new husband. The last time I'd seen my sister, I'd asked her to show me a photograph of her stepfather, and she'd replied, 'Yuck, why would I take a photo of him?' That was as much as I could get out of her about the new marriage, and no one else was forthcoming.

Once she moved in with us, my sister's presence dominated the household. It wasn't that Zoe was demanding or a drama queen, only that her life seemed more centrestage than ours. Jake and I became bit players, always hanging about on the edges. Not big enough to be properly involved, but big enough to notice we weren't. It was an odd sensation, to suddenly become a supporting actor in my own life. My world turned on its head. Zoe had always had star quality, but now she was the star.

On top of this, my sister observed unpleasant things about me that other people didn't. Reflected back at me in Zoe's ever-present gaze was my own badness. She cornered me whenever the adults were gone.

'Jess, I saw what you just did.' She seemed to materialise out of the surrounding air. 'You can't control the game like that. You can't make Jake play all the roles you don't want.'

'But I'm not.' Tears pricked behind my eyes. 'This is the game. It goes like this.'

Zoe smiled. 'You're *so* bossy! You think that no one notices, but I do. Your mum lets you get away with anything. Poor Jakey! I won't let you get away with it, Jess, even if everyone else does.'

'But he always wants to play with me. I don't make him play!'

Zoe turned to Jake, putting an arm around his shoulder. 'Jakey, do you think Jessie is bossy?'

Jake looked from me to Zoe and back again. 'It's okay,' he said finally.

'See! He's frightened to say so, but he does.'

Defeated, I ran out into the garden and climbed into the comforting bough of my favourite tree. Wrapping my arms about myself, I willed back tears. Later, when all was forgotten, I crept inside still throbbing with emotion. I was careful after Zoe came to live with us, careful and alert. I raised my guard like a shield, watching with sideways glances, waiting for her to pounce.

Did Zoe's defence of Jake, her vigilant patrolling of my bossiness, allow him to come out of his shell? After all this time, it's hard to say. He seemed as intimidated by her as I was, and certainly not interested in aligning himself with her against me. My brother has always been a gentle soul, seeing other people's hurts, not taking offence. I suspect that if he'd had his way, he'd have liked us all to get along.

≈

At school, my nose began to bleed on a daily basis. Sitting in class, suddenly there'd be a bright drip on my schoolbook. My teacher would take one look at me and point to the door. Outside, blood rushed over the cement and I tried various different techniques to stem the flow. Years later it struck me that perhaps this daily nosebleed was a response to my sister's sudden presence in the house. Before, Billie and Zoe had come and gone. I only had to be wary of them for short periods. But when Zoe moved in, I felt under constant surveillance. The parameters of my existence shifted. I was no longer the firstborn, no longer queen bee. Any authority I had washed away in her company, and the longer she stayed, the worse it seemed to get.

At the dinner table one night, Zoe announced something she'd heard I'd said at school.

'Apparently, Jessie has been telling her friends she doesn't like me.'

It was true that I often felt that way, but I was fairly sure I'd never said so. I racked my brain for who I might have told, but there was no one. The other kids thought my sister was Madonna, and I knew I wouldn't find a receptive audience for my complaints, even if I'd been willing to share them.

'I didn't,' I stuttered out. 'I ... wouldn't.'

'So, now you're lying.' Zoe turned to our father. 'Dad, now she's *lying*.'

It mortified me that my sister would accuse me this way, but deep down I was terrified that she could somehow read my mind.

'I'm not lying,' I said. 'I didn't say that.'

'Yeah, but you think it, don't you?' My sister smirked. She seemed to be enjoying herself.

I was bewildered. If Zoe knew I didn't say it, why did she say I did?

My father sighed. 'Jess, don't talk about Zoe at school, okay?' Not really listening.

33

I wanted so much for my sister to like me, but how could that happen if she saw all my badness? If she was able to read my mind? If she knew how angry I often felt? I tried hard to keep my hurt feelings stashed away where no one could see them, but my nose bled every day like clockwork, as though my body had no other way of dispersing the intensity of my unsettled emotions.

Sometimes when my friends from school came over, they asked, 'Do you think we can get your sister to play?'

I sighed, knowing what it would mean. My friends were too starstruck to speak to Zoe, so it would be me who had to ask. I didn't even want her to play, because it always involved some degree of humiliation for me, but peer pressure being what it was, I went ahead and asked. Standing at the doorway to her room, my friends in a little crowd at my back, I made my request. Zoe's response was always the same. She'd smile sweetly at us, and then say, 'Yes, I'll play, but only if you—Jessie—only if you say, *Zoe is the bestest, most beautiful, kindest, most generous, most amazing sister in the whole world and I love her more than anyone else.*'

Of course, Zoe only asked me to say that because she knew I wouldn't want to, or that if I did say it, it wouldn't be true. So what she was actually asking was that I lie in front of my friends—lie and grovel—and most of the time I wouldn't be able to. I would outright refuse, and Zoe would nonchalantly say, 'Oh, I won't be able to play then,' and my friends would all be cross. They'd hiss, 'Just say it. Why can't you say it?'

But I couldn't, because it just wasn't true.

≈

I never experienced Billie and Zoe as little children. Years later, staring at my sisters' baby photos, I try to fit how I first remember them—grown-up and awe-inspiring—with their slant-eyed baby smiles. We still have some of my sisters' photo albums. In one, entitled *Billie 69–71*, Billie has scrawled on the title page in childish handwriting, *Daughter of two families*. Listed in two separate columns are the names of each family member, including pets. In contrast, in Zoe's album, which has no title, Zoe has gone through and cut out figures from half the photographs, excising them from the proof of her life. It's impossible for me to tell who they once were, though I am pleased that— as far as I can see—the missing figures are too large to be me. My mother tells me that from the moment Zoe knew my mother was pregnant with me, she was enraged. Through the very act of being conceived, I became the usurper. Zoe was five years old, and I was yet to be born, but we'd gotten off on the wrong foot right from the beginning.

≈

It's possible to love and hate someone with equal intensity. I hated the way Zoe needled me, but—more than anything—I wanted to be close to her. Studying my sister carefully, I wondered at her dazzling force. Zoe tick-tacked down the walkway on her skateboard at breakneck speed, her voice welling in song. I watched, holding my breath, as she jumped from the board, landing gracefully on her feet on the pebbled driveway as though no great feat had been accomplished. And when my sister was not there to see, Jake and I copied her skateboard manoeuvres with little success but endless enthusiasm.

Zoe sang, loud and fierce and full, and Jake and I crept nearer. We were afraid of her, but she drew us closer, like puppies to the bright, spark-spitting fireside. Zoe could cartwheel, do the splits, walk on her hands and stand up on a surfboard in the big waves. When she came home from the beach, brown and sand-encrusted in her bikini, she let me rub moisturising cream onto her smooth, hard back.

'Can I get the cream? You want me to?' How I longed for her to acknowledge my usefulness.

'Yeah, all right, Jess.'

Zoe lay face down and naked on the couch. Scrambling onto her back, I squirted the cream out in wriggly pinkish lines. I sat astride her brown body, concentrating on the disappearing swirls of cream beneath my fingertips. Slowly, I smoothed the cream into the skin of this mysterious big sister, wondering at all her burnished perfection, counting her random moles and freckles, dreaming of the time when I too should be so divine. Zoe had a birthmark on the back of her thigh, in the elongated shape of Australia, like she'd been marked out for something. Something special. My sister was calm in these moments, and I squeezed on more and more cream until finally I could say I had covered every inch of her, and climbed off, triumphant and shining.

≈

My mother's two silver bangles were the first thing she put on after waking. They were chunky, but worn smooth by everyday wear, and they made a melodic clinking sound as she went through her day. I found the sound soothing, and it meant I always knew where she was. Often all she wore was a sarong, not even tied together, just wrapped around her and tucked in at the top. As a small child this didn't bother me, but once I reached school age, it made me self-conscious. I knew she was always naked underneath, and I feared the sarong falling off at inopportune moments. When my mother walked us to the bus stop at the end of our driveway in the mornings, I made her hide behind a tree at the first sound of the bus. She obliged, unconcerned by my embarrassment but willing to respect it. To be fair, this laxness around clothing was normal in my early childhood, and most of my peers have similar memories—a collective horror of our mothers' loose sarongs.

Much of the gardening work my mother did in the nude—especially the raking, which was never-ending—and Jake and I were always on guard for unexpected visitors. Often it was tradesmen, and we'd call out in exasperation, 'Mum, the plumber's here. Where's your sarong?'

My mother never seemed hurried or alarmed, but we'd try to keep the bloke talking until she'd gotten herself covered. I was less concerned about my father's nakedness, because generally he wore a pair of underpants, which we considered 'clothes'. But he always did a nude dash down the walkway after a shower, his penis jiggling while he jogged. When I was little this seemed fine, not even really noteworthy, but once I got bigger it was the cause of some consternation. I didn't understand why my father couldn't wrap himself in a towel. When my friends stayed they were all alert to the potential of this naked run. 'Is your dad in the bathroom?' they'd ask, pointing at the door. If he was, they'd vacate the vicinity. Sometimes, though, they'd knock on the bathroom door, thinking it was free, and my father would cheerily call, 'I'm coming out!' And whichever luckless friend it was would let out a little squeal and rush away. My father was oblivious, waving to us as he jiggled past.

≈

One of my favourite games with Jake was dress-ups, specifically me dressing him. Always obliging, he donned skirts and resigned himself to pigtails, tottering around in a pair of someone's old high heels. I liked him to pretend to be my own personal dolly, and sometimes Zoe would spring this game on me.

'Can I dress you up like a geisha girl, Jess?'

There was, in fact, nothing I'd like more.

I waited in anticipation while she collected up the bits and pieces that would be my makeshift costume. Sitting still, as instructed, lifting my face—eyes closed in rapture—while she smoothed on my makeup. Under Zoe's fingertips I was becoming something other. Jake would stand by, watching, the tables finally turned. I was now the dolly and he was fetch-and-carry boy.

'Can you throw me that tie, Jakey?' Zoe asked. 'And hold this bit tight?'

When she finished she inspected her work, self-critical as always.

'The lips are a bit crooked.' She grasped my chin, turning my head from side to side. 'But you look pretty cute.'

A wild happiness would burst in my chest. I had done something right! I glanced across at Jake and he was flushed with pleasure too. I was the dolly and he was the helper and Zoe was pleased with her work. When she was done with us we'd scurry off to continue the game, our hearts filled with dizzy lightness.

≈

In Zoe's first year in Burringbar we watched as she grew and grew and grew. She wasn't tall like Billie, but her school uniform pressed in upon her and was soon busting at the seams. At fourteen Zoe was skinny and straight-bodied, and then suddenly she was curved. My mother too saw the sudden shortness of her skirts, her uniform tight under the arms and growing firm across her budding breasts.

'Do you want me to take you into town to get a new school dress, Zoe?' my mother asked, but Zoe shook her head, her lip lifting in the corner in a quirking secret smile.

My sister went to the dresser drawer and fished around for some safety pins, pinning up the burst seams of her school dress.

Watching her, my mother pressed her lips together in a firm line, but our father only smiled, as though the thought of his safety-pinned and beautiful daughter brought him an easy kind of joy.

Zoe was in the school musical, and Jake and I went with our parents to see her perform. We sat in the hard-backed plastic seats, wriggling with impatience until Zoe walked on stage, all brightness and spark. When she sang I wanted to stand on my chair and yell, *She's my sister! She's mine!*

There were boys sitting behind us, and when Zoe appeared they whispered among themselves, and I strained to hear.

'Look at her—she's so hot.'

'Have you seen the safety pins?'

'Yeah, hot. I'd have her any day.'

My face burned and I turned around to watch the boys through the cracks between the seats. Leaning down, their heads close together in whispered communion, they looked up at Zoe on stage through flopping fringes, with stark, heavy stares. I was entranced. A strange kind of blush crept up from deep inside me, quickening my heart and reddening my cheeks. My mother touched her fingertips to my shoulders and I knew that I was to face the front.

'Mum, did you hear those boys?' I whispered.

'Zoe's singing, Jess—you going to watch?'

I leaned forward and peered around at my father's face. He grinned, a knowing kind of smile, and I knew then that they had both heard.

'I want to tell them it's us. Can I?'

'No, Jess. Sshh. Watch the show.'

Turning back to the stage, I watched my *hot* sister sing, and Zoe's voice broke over me in waves. I forgot the boys behind us. I forgot everything then but the soaring force of my sister's song.

A few days later, Zoe came home with a mohawk. A bona fide punk. Most mornings she shaved the sides of her head bald with a disposable razor. If I was quiet, she let me sit on the edge of the bath to watch. Zoe had one brown mole on her head and every day she sliced the top off with the razor and blood ran down in a red stripe. To her end-of-year formal she wore a strapless, netted, multicoloured fluorescent tutu when everyone else was still wearing taffeta. With her mohawk and her tutu and her muscular, nimble, cartwheeling body and all her magnificent bellowing songs, how else would I see her than as a real-life pop star? Alluring, enchanting, but aloof. Always just out of reach.

≈

Since I was small, I've had a repeated conversation that goes: 'Your mother's always been such a beautiful woman.' Meaningful pause. 'You look so much like your dad.' With almost a tut-tut, as though this lack of genetic inheritance was mysteriously my fault, or—at the very least—something to be ashamed of. Whenever I reported this conversation back to my mother, she seemed deeply affronted and said, 'Oh, but your father is so handsome!'

Children don't care about their parents' beauty, or perhaps

they just find it difficult to judge, but my mother was the type of beautiful that never went unremarked. She had long, honey-coloured hippie-hair, parted down the middle, and eyes so light green they seemed almost translucent. When properly clothed, she wore long skirts that she made herself from geometric batik cloth. She had dozens of them, like a uniform. Every Christmas my father bought her an ankle-length white embroidered skirt with a matching white embroidered singlet, and she would wear them that one day to please him, and then never again—until the next Christmas, when the whole ritual would play out once more.

My mother has always had an enigmatic air. When I was a child she appeared utterly self-contained. Not emotionless or uncaring, just quietly self-sufficient. She was receptive to my approaches, and always a good listener, but she didn't give much away. As I grew older, I realised that I didn't know a single thing about her from before I was born. My mother had no stories, no past. Once this became apparent, I crept into her bed when she was reading and confessed my lack of knowledge. She looked surprised, but she smiled, as though it was nice I'd finally noticed. I lay down beside her and she switched off the light. Under the cover of that darkness my mother asked, 'What do you want to know?' I whispered a series of questions. Anything that came to mind. I asked her if she'd had boyfriends before my dad. I asked her how she'd felt about them. I asked her where she'd lived and what she used to do with her time. I asked her where she'd travelled, and with who. I asked her the names of her childhood friends, her pets. I asked her about her siblings, her parents, her grandparents. My mother answered all these questions, but I woke up the next morning feeling as though nothing was any clearer. Even though I had the facts—or some of them at least—my mother still felt completely unknown to me, as though this mysteriousness was a fundamental quality of who she was.

I knew far more about my father than I did about my mother, though he didn't talk about his past much either. Like my mother, he didn't tell stories—he was just more upfront about his inner workings. I knew that he didn't get along with his father, that they didn't have any kind of relationship. I'd gathered he felt disappointed by his mother, that he didn't believe she was capable of loving him. He'd told me he'd grown up, at least for some of his childhood, in a country town, and that for some reason at some stage he'd been sent off to live with a relative. I knew he thought his parents had been restrictive—or unwelcoming—regarding who he felt himself to be. Sometimes my father talked to us about his work, or his beliefs around his work. He spoke about how many of his patients were held back or stuck or stagnated because they couldn't cut ties with very destructive family members. How a lot of the time he wished he could just say to his patients, 'Don't speak to your mother anymore.' For him, cutting ties was the simplest solution.

≈

There was one boy who Zoe liked more than the others. The night the family met him she came and dropped down beside me on the couch in a sighing sprawl.

'Did you see his eyebrows, Jess?' She smiled at me with the full force of her gaze and I was momentarily stunned. I felt myself fill with such a sudden weightlessness that I thought I might cry.

She talked to me! About a boy!

This small moment of union between two sisters offered a glimpse of possibilities I hadn't yet known.

The boy visited our house, and I watched as Zoe and he sidestepped each other's hearts. Older—eighteen to Zoe's fourteen—sometimes the boy was not where he said he would be. Once, when he came to visit, Zoe disappeared before his arrival, galloping off on her horse and not returning until dusk. He waited and waited and I watched and watched, until finally he got up and stalked away, hitchhiking the long way home.

Our father shook his head with irritation. 'They're playing games with each other.'

'What type of game is it, Daddy?' I was confused.

'It's not a good game,' my father sighed. 'Sometimes adults play games with each other, but someone always gets hurt.'

I thought about my father's words but I didn't understand them. I didn't understand why Zoe would leave before the boy arrived or why he'd leave before Zoe returned. It was a tawdry kind of game. *An adult game.* When Zoe returned from her horseride, sweaty and tired, our father gave her a talk about

44

responsibility. I watched as my sister stormed away, her face red and blurred with tears. The afternoon became quiet then, and even the sounds of the birds calling seemed to fade into the oncoming dark.

≈

The primary school bus got home a good hour before the high school bus, giving Jake and me a snatch of time before Zoe arrived where things were the same as they used to be. We liked to fossick in the creek straight after school. Gathering up kitchen strainers and a few jars, we'd head down the rainforest steps to catch and collect the tiny creek creatures. My mother let us play down there unattended, though we knew she peered over the banks from time to time, checking on our whereabouts. Sometimes she'd call out and we'd call back and then she'd leave us to it.

Catching creatures with kitchen strainers was often a game of chance. It was hard to see what was beneath the water. You just swiped down and hoped for the best. Speedy-bugs were common but hard to secure. Tadpoles were slow swimmers but infrequent finds. Shrimps were ever-present, not even worth bothering with. Guppies were a bit of a prize. Miniature blue yabbies under rocks were like diamonds. We'd pop all these creatures in our jars, creating mini-aquariums with a few hand-picked pebbles and scattered creek weed.

'What'd you get?' my brother would ask.

'Just a few shrimps,' I'd shrug.

It was a conflict-free zone. We didn't feel particularly propri-etorial about our finds, often filling up each other's jars. We tipped all the creatures back in before dark anyway. They didn't survive long outside the creek. Perhaps this was our small way of world building? Tiny environments we could control, if only for an hour or two. And every day was a new day. You never knew what you might find. Any small rock could yield a prized blue yabby. So many rocks in the creek, just waiting to be upturned.

≈

In the evenings, my sister would often seek my father out for some kind of conversation over dinner, but it always went awry.

'Dad, yesterday on the radio on the bus,' Zoe said, 'I heard that eighty per cent of Americans don't have access to free medical care. Like, if they get hurt they can't just go to hospital. Don't you think that's shit? I mean, America's supposed to be the leader of the free world!'

'Eighty per cent?' our father queried, unsmiling.

The light in the kitchen was warm beneath the stained-glass lampshade. My mother placed saucepans of curry on the table and spooned out servings of rice. Jake and I sat side by side with our small wooden bowls. Too little for curry, we ate rice smeared with tangy yogurt. Our father put a forkload of curry into his mouth, and then breathed out in a flustered puff because it was too hot.

'Is it too spicy?' my mother asked.

'No, no—it's just temperature-hot.'

Our father wiped his mouth with a tea towel and sipped slowly from his wineglass.

Zoe persisted. 'Well, maybe not eighty per cent exactly, Dad, but—'

'Maybe you should make sure you get your facts straight,' my father interrupted, 'before you start telling us what you think about American politics.'

Out of Billie's shadow, Zoe had *opinions* and *ideas*, and Jake and I sat still, compelled by the certainty in her voice, while our father slowly picked apart her theories over dinner and displayed them to her, mangled, on a platter. We watched as Zoe's distress seemed to envelop the whole room. Our father would not budge. Though he loved Zoe and all her momentous feeling, he could never let her win. Nearly grown, my sister swung between elation and despair. One single hint of impatience from our father, and we watched as she crashed down as though from the greatest height, plummeting at high speed. Unaware of the vastness of these hurtling falls, my father continued on oblivious. Zoe was no sun to his earth, and though he saw her ripen and bloom, he seemed unsurprised. Her beauty, her vital gleaming force—*a fact*—not worth a remark, and what to say anyway? Again and again Zoe plummeted, crestfallen, waiting for that one sentence from our father that would reveal her as worthy, as integral to his life.

47

Nearing adolescence, I watched this dynamic play out and thought, *She knows what Dad's going to say. She knows he's going to cut her down, so why does she keep going back?*

Lately, I've been thinking a lot about thirst—how for some people it seems unquenchable. But there is no thirst if you're not dehydrated, right? I can only assume that for my sister to go back again and again, seeking my father's approval, she didn't feel that she had it. She was thirsty. And perhaps that's how I was with her. Always yearning for something she would never give, but— ever hopeful—going back again and again to try.

≈

In her final year of high school Billie asked to leave Sydney, and her private school scholarship, and move to Burringbar to begin again. Standing in the doorway of the study, I watched as my father spoke to her on the phone. His voice was soft, and I longed to know what it was she said.

The sound of Zoe singing in her bedroom drifted down the walkway, distracting me from my father's words. I restrained myself from stepping further inside the study to listen. It was hard for me to understand why Billie would want to leave her other life. I knew the girls' mother had a new baby, although— despite multiple requests—I was yet to see a photograph. When my father hung up he went to find my mother. I trailed after him, unravelling my school-plaited hair.

My mother stood at the kitchen bench mixing spices for

dinner. My father told her what Billie wanted.

Wiping her hands on a tea towel, my mother tucked her long hair behind her ear, glancing sideways at me. 'But what about Zoe?' she asked softly. 'She just seems to be settling into it all.'

'I know,' my father sighed. 'It felt like a good thing that the two of them were separate for a bit.'

In the paper at six for having the reading age of a thirteen-year-old, Billie had always been something of an over-achiever. Not just at school but at everything. When they were side by side, it had seemed constantly that Billie achieved while Zoe lacked. The daily grind of being second; the eternal lesson of siblinghood.

'And what about Billie's scholarship?' my mother asked.

'She says she doesn't care about it anymore.'

My father wondered, in the beginning, whether it was just a whim. But when Billie rang again, her voice soft and broken on the end of the line, he relented.

'We can't say yes to one and not the other,' he said, walking outside and leaning down to pull out some weeds that had sprung up in the garden.

I wondered what it would be like having two sisters live with us instead of one.

≈

When Billie came to live in Burringbar there were six of us. We became a Big Family, and Jake and I stepped back to watch

49

our sisters' lives. My mother made Billie a long, billowing blue school skirt, and when she rode her bike in the mornings to catch a lift to her extra physics class, it flapped like a sail behind her. Billie was elegant and grown up, stylish and worldly, with short cropped hair and certain eyes. Academic and effortlessly popular, she was quickly voted captain of the local rural high school. Billie swept back into Zoe's life, leaving her sidelined and quiet.

Both girls began dancing classes. My mother drove them after school along a winding mountain road to a country hall where they danced and sweated and competed. Jake and I came for the drive, a dragging afternoon, and I was shocked by the big girls' lithe bodies and their sleek, fluid movements. Copying their steps, I was hopelessly lost and out of time. After a few weeks of slapdash effort I resigned myself to the plastic chairs with Jake. Watching Billie and Zoe dance, I pushed aside all hope of such proficiency to another time and place, to the years ahead when I would be grown.

Standing at the rim of womanhood, staring in, I watched my sisters traverse the terrain and longed to join them. Two long-limbed, taut-bodied queens—regal and sure. There was no hint of the spotty heartbreak, the self-consciousness, the triviality that would prove later to be my teenage world. I saw only their magnificence.

The theatre of them.

The colour, whirl and sparkle.

One afternoon, my parents picked Jake and me up from school to take us to the beach. A treat. A surprise-afternoon-beach-trip, exciting for all its foreign allure. We waited at primary school with the other kids, hot and tired, and then swelled with joy as our sisters' faces appeared, unexpected, at the car windows. Zoe jumped out and shimmied her way around the car to the bonnet. She lounged on the front of the car, dressed for maximum impact and embarrassment, short skirt and funky sunglasses, playing at movie seduction.

'Jakey! Jessie!' Zoe called loudly, pointing at us. With the poise of a teenage starlet, she crooked her finger and beckoned us to the car. Billie poked her head from the window, pouting. My brother and I stood frozen between uncertainty and glee. Sidelong glances showed the waiting kids were as impressed as we were.

'Come on, you two little spunk machines! Let's go!'

We grabbed our bags and ran for the car, faces ducked to smother our smiles. My sisters grinned, embarrassment accomplished, and Zoe reached out and tousled Jake's floppy hair as he climbed past and into the back seat.

At the beach the wind whipped about, blowing against our skin until it itched. The shoreline was long and curved. My sisters laid towels out, and stripped to get that all-over tan. Topless and coppery, sprawled out in their beauty—I was dazed by their daring, their pluck. A line of them—with my mother too—all beaming and aglow. And one day I would join the line. I examined them as though seeing my future, cataloguing every detail. The languid shift of my mother's limbs, the soft curl of Zoe's lip when she caught a boy watching her, the way Billie stretched her legs before she stood and walked to the water. Mesmerised, I memorised their movements, and waited for my time to come.

≈

The girls had large teenage parties in the house. Our parents retreated to their bedroom to give them space. Jake and I were supposed to stay away but we always snuck out to watch. Pressing our noses against the glass doors, we peered in, our breath misting up the glass, leaving the world before us foggy and strange. The big kids played spin the bottle, and they kissed, frightening long kisses, and sometimes Billie and Zoe slipped Jake and me inside the circle to play. When it was my turn, I watched the end of the bottle rotate, slow and hypnotic, and when finally it stopped I hid my eyes from where it landed.

'Come on, Jess, you've got to kiss him now!'

Blindly, I rushed over to plant a quick kiss on the unknown boy's rough cheek, my heart pounding. Billie and Zoe laughed and cheered, and I blushed, a deep red.

At the girls' parties there was music and dancing, staged and theatrical, and there were more games—dares and contests. Dressed up extravagantly, my sisters were the centre of it all, and they ran the party like a circus. They were entertainers, they were ringmasters, and I was awed by their glittering routine.

But in a little while my mother called us to bed, and Jake and I went, clean teeth and pyjamas. We slept in the same island room, our beds coupled at a right angle in the corner, our pillows pushed together and our hair intertwining. Tucking us in, our mother said goodnight, then closed the door to the garden outside. Left alone, we whispered together and Jake's silences shortened. In the dark of the bedroom, my brother spoke with no stoppers. We lay relaxed but wakeful, gazing through the large windows at the jungle palms in the moonlight, words sliding from our tongues like the water down the rapids.

The future stretched out before us, bright with expectation. It was quiet in our bedroom, the strains of the big girls' party only faintly filtering in. I reached my hand beneath my pillow and slid my fingers against Jake's floppy silk-like hair, the texture of it so different from my own coarse, wavy locks. Jake reached up and softly gripped my arm and we grasped hands beneath the pillow—a singular fist, tight with togetherness—until sleep came at last and grabbed us in a sudden slip into that other, dream-filled darkness.

≈

With the big girls in Burringbar, I imagined their mother and their other family living all that way away. I wondered how it was that they had two of everything and I had only one. Two mothers, two fathers, two sisters and two brothers.

'Why did Billie want to come up here to live, Mum?' I asked.

'Well, when her mother had the new baby, I think she felt left out,' my mother said carefully. 'Billie said when she went places in the car with them, they seemed like a proper family and she felt on the outside. She said it was in the car that she felt the saddest.'

'But the new baby was her brother. How could she be left out?'

'Sometimes when a baby comes it's hard not to feel like that, even when everyone tries really hard to make sure that everybody feels a part of the family.'

My mother's words didn't make sense to me, but I stored them somewhere inside to bring out and mull over later.

'Is the baby our brother too? How come we don't get to see him?'

'He's not related by blood, and he lives in Sydney.'

'But Billie and Zoe are our half-sisters, and he's their half-brother, so he must be our quarter-brother, right?'

'No, he's not related by blood.'

'How come, Mum?'

'You and the girls have the same father. The girls and the new baby have the same mother. It's separate.'

'Well, I still think he's a little bit related. I want to meet him.'

I struggled to comprehend the difference between my sisters' lives and my own. The world seemed to revolve around Billie and Zoe. It was brighter where they stood. These grown-up girls inhabited a place where everything *happened*, where there was no waiting, where things moved. Their world was wide and deep and free, where mine was small and enclosed. The possibility that Billie or Zoe felt on the outside of anything was perplexing and unfathomable.

≈

Often when my father got home from work he sat at the kitchen table and told my mother about his day. Sometimes, after just one look at his face, my mother would close the door to the kitchen so that we wouldn't hear, and we would know he'd had a difficult time at work, and we should do our best to stay away. All my father's patients had his home number, and quite frequently they called. He'd tried to train Jake and me to answer the phone by saying, 'Dr Cole's residence. Who is speaking?' And then we were supposed to say, 'I'll just go and see if he is here,' so my father would have a choice to speak or not. But we were untrainable, and what we usually said was, 'Hello? I'll just check if he says he's here,' or some version of that, which never failed to enrage my father, though we couldn't be persuaded of the seriousness of the situation. We didn't know that mostly when his patients called it was because they were thinking about suicide, and it was his job to talk them back from the brink. Some patients called a lot, and we got used to them and knew their names. I can still hear the fragility of those voices, hanging there on the other end of the line.

'Is your father there?' A broken, ragged breath. 'Can I speak to him?'

≈

Holidaying on the weekend at the coast, the family went to a friend's house for dinner. Our father drank and drank, his voice becoming slurred, until finally my mother urged him from the kitchen and back to the hotel. It was late by then and we all stumbled off to bed, but my parents' voices were loud through the thin hotel walls.

At home, snuggled up with Jake in our island bedroom, I rarely heard them fight. That night my father's tone was hard and my mother whispered in reply, high-pitched and shrill. It seemed my father was angry and my mother sad, an awful harassed sadness. More than anything, I wanted to go to them and be comforted, but the harshness of my father's voice forbade me.

Lying awake, I listened to the hissing, rebounding sounds of their argument and wondered where I could go. My brother lay sleeping beside me, his mouth open and slack. I wanted to wake him so I wouldn't be alone, but I knew he'd be frightened too. Jake would look to me with sleep-fogged eyes, asking to be told that it was all right, and I would have to say that it was. I thought of Billie and Zoe sleeping in the next room, but could not decide which one of them would not reject me if I came and woke her in the dark. My sisters were equally daunting, and equally likely to rebuff. Finally I chose, tiptoeing out the door and into the girls' room.

Standing at the foot of Billie's bed, I watched her sleep-softened face and then slowly climbed up on the mattress, touching her calf.

Stirring, Billie sat up sleepily. 'Jess, what's wrong, baby?'

I inched up closer, trembling a little. 'Mum and Dad are fighting. I can hear them.'

Dropping my head then, I cried, a frightened muffled cry. Reaching out, Billie rubbed both her palms briskly along my forearms, pressing her forehead up to my face and smiling into my eyes.

'Come on, Jess. It's all right.'

'Do you think they'll split up?'

'Oh, Jess—don't worry, it's not that bad. It's just an argument. Come and lie with me, in my bed.' Billie lifted her covers for me to climb under, and I snuggled in beside her.

'Are you sure they won't split up?'

'It'd have to get a lot worse than this. And for longer.'

I wondered how my sister knew these things. The shadow of her other life.

'Billie, how come you wanted to live up here?'

'Just wanted something new, I suppose.' Billie sighed, and I glanced at her face in the dark. 'It was lonely in Sydney without Zoe, lonelier than I thought it would be.'

It was hard to imagine Billie lonely.

'But I'll go to university next year, so I'll be back in Sydney again for a while. Not for long, though—Australia's too small for me. When I finish uni I'm going to live in a really big city like London or New York or Tokyo.'

'In another country?'

'It's a crazy big world.'

'What about Zoe? What'll she do?'

'She's moving back to Mum's next year too. Finish school down there. Go to drama school, maybe. NIDA. If she can get in. You have to be really good to get into drama school, so I don't know if she will.'

'Zoe will be famous one day.' Of this I was sure. 'A famous singer.'

I imagined all I knew of big cities: cars, people and tall buildings. In my mind I saw Billie and Zoe on a picnic with their mother and baby brother, lazing around in the sunshine on the steps of the Opera House, seagulls fluttering upwards into the sky.

'How long have you been awake, Jess?'

'Since we came home.'

'Ages, hey? Well, you better go to sleep or you'll be tired tomorrow. We're going to the beach, remember. You don't want to be too tired to come out with Zoe and me.'

I turned over and Billie wrapped her long body around my small frame. A gentle spooning. Safe and comforted in my biggest sister's embrace, I lay awake and stared across the room at Zoe's sleep-tossed sheets and splayed brown limbs. I knew soon these mysterious sisters would be gone. Soon they would be *adults*. Bold and brave, they would go to face the world. Watching the fitful dreams of my other, less trusted sister, I drifted in and out of an uneasy, restless sleep.

≈

And just like that, Billie and Zoe, who'd dominated our world so completely, suddenly moved on. Without the big girls in Burringbar, the house was quiet. My nose stopped randomly bleeding and things settled into their old familiar pace. And though I sometimes missed the excitement of my sisters' presence, my relief at their departure was palpable. Freed from vigilance, I found myself relaxing, and all the ways I'd been unsatisfactory seemed to matter less. With Billie and Zoe gone, I became, again, the centre of my own existence. We were back to being a Small Family, and Jake and I were left to our own devices. We picked up our games from where we'd left off, though I'd been humbled. In birth I was the usurper, but in life I'd been thoroughly usurped. Probably I was still bossy, my eleven-year-old self still learning how to give and take. But I asked my brother more questions, checking in to see if I'd read his needs right. Before, I had believed his enthusiasm was a given. After being schooled by my sisters, I thought it best to confirm.

On that verge between childhood and what came next, Jake and I began to seek out places beyond the range of the adults. Under the cover of overhanging trees, a ridge of land grew from our front garden like an arm thrown out in sleep. In its meandering journey, the creek had shaped and carved it, creating a thin strip of unharnessed ground that dropped away sharply at either side. It appeared to point, like a finger, to some kind of destination, but instead ended abruptly in a tapering muddy slope. Below was a secret place, not accessible except by sliding down the mud. The adults never went there. A large tree had capsized down on the flats below the ridge, and Jake and I made the exposed roots our hideaway. We slithered down the slope and settled into the tree's arms, playing intricate games in the tangled caverns of its roots. Tiny imagined houses and tunnelled pathways, infinite worlds that exploded in our minds until the whole upturned tree teemed with life.

'Where've you been?' my mother would ask on our return. 'I couldn't find you.'

'Down the ridge,' I'd say, vaguely.

'What were you doing down there?'

'Just playing in the tree.' I shrugged my shoulders. It was hard to explain.

'You okay, Jakey?' she'd ask. 'Was it fun?'

He nodded, smiling, but he had nothing else to add.

In that time, Jake and I stuck to the things we had always loved: the creek, the beach, our pets, our little gang of friends, all those detailed imaginary games. We weren't ready to fly—but with the departure of our sisters, we had room at last to flex our wings.

≈

My brother Jake had always had a proficiency in areas I did not. Drawing, a talent that was much prized in our household, was something he did so well from an early age that his pictures were often given special treatment, or at least a more adult critique. When Jake took up playing the guitar it was obvious from the outset that it was going to be his thing. His skill was quickly prodigious; in no time at all he could pluck out the melodies of the theme songs to all our afternoon television shows. A neat party trick. Perhaps, even then, what Jake liked about music was that it gave him another kind of voice. He could express things in melody that he'd struggled to do in words. As the youngest, he'd often been overshadowed. Three older sisters. But once he found the guitar he was very rarely without it, and some part of himself that he had kept hidden began to unfurl. He was less shy, less quiet. Of course, in our family he'd have to fight for the limelight, but he was gathering skills at a disconcerting speed.

≈

Our primary school had always been an odd mix of things. Before the arrival of the hippies, Burringbar was peopled by a bunch of longstanding local families, old-fashioned and traditional. When I started kindergarten there were about sixty kids in the whole school, but in my final year there were more than a hundred and sixty. With the influx of new settlers, things had been shaken up. Considering the radical nature of what these new arrivals had brought with them—drugs, nudity, flexible relationship arrangements, just to name a few—the old guard had been relatively open-minded. The teachers did seem to see us as two distinct groups: those who had head lice and those who didn't. On nit-checking days, we were separated along those lines, and often the hippie-kids were put into the nit-group as a matter of course. Lice don't discriminate, so generally we were all itchy, and those in the nit-group felt this arbitrary division to be an injustice. The kids were less judgmental, and at school my peers usually hung out in one ragtag group—though I did once have a local girl say, 'Oh, I can't play with you today because I only play with my cousins.' Of whom, of course, there were many.

Outside of school Jake and I still mostly spent time with the children of our parents' friends. We ran together in packs, climbing trees, swinging from the Tarzan vines, splashing our way through the creeks. Going out bush with baskets of fruit from the orchard, we played elaborate games, laughing, bickering and making up again. I'm supposing all the kids from local families spent weekends with their cousins, but as we got older there were occasional instances of crossover, and one of the girls would ask me to stay the night at her house. I loved the ordered nature of these strange suburban sleepovers. These friends had wall-to-wall carpeting, sometimes in pink. They had exotic dinners like sausages and mash. Every night they had dessert. Their mothers laid out the outfits they were to wear the next day on their beds. There were rules and strict routines. Everything ran like clockwork. I came home feeling deeply disenchanted about the black slate and Persian rugs on our floors. More than anything I wanted to be able to roll around on that luscious wall-to-wall carpeting.

'But Mum, you can lie down anywhere and it's comfortable,' I'd say, longingly.

My mother just shook her head. My parents had fled the suburban aesthetic of their own childhoods as though it was actually toxic, and our house was all earthen colours and geometric designs. To me, it seemed so ordinary, so drab, so unglamorous. Our house had no sparkle, no lace, no frills, and I yearned potently for its opposite. I don't think I wanted to be 'normal', it was more that I saw these local girls' houses as deeply foreign, and hence alluring. I entered those spaces wide-eyed at the suburban splendour.

On top of this, a self-consciousness about my parents' choices was starting to leak in. Hanging around on a street corner after school as an almost-teenager, I spotted my father doing a lap of town, ghetto-blaster on his shoulder, wearing his bright yellow Esprit shirt, on an afternoon errand.

Glimpsing him in the distance, I hoped he wouldn't come my way.

'Isn't that ... your dad?' my tittering friends asked. When he jogged right past calling, 'Hi, Possum!', it was a hard question to evade.

'What's he doing?'

Now, I suspect he was rushing about trying to get that beloved ghetto-blaster repaired, and jogging with it on his shoulder was just a natural time-management strategy, but the yellow women's Esprit T-shirt was harder to explain.

My father loved that shirt. '*Esprit* is French for spirit!' he'd proclaim. 'S-P-I-R-I-T! You know, spirit, life, strength. That's me!'

'But why does it have to be bright yellow?'

'That's my favourite colour!'

'But it's a girl's shirt, Dad.'

All I got in response was a slight roll of the eyes. For my father, gendered clothing was irrelevant.

There were advantages to growing up in a family with a high tolerance for eccentricity. Boundaries were loose, undefined. Odd fashion choices were celebrated, experimental artworks were encouraged, and socially inappropriate expressions of authenticity were never shunned or derided. But sometimes—especially out in public—I was starting to wish my parents played by the rules.

≈

Billie was at uni in Sydney, ensconced in her own life. We rarely heard from her. She had well and truly flown the nest. Zoe had moved back to her mother's, finished school and started uni, but a little while in she hatched a plan to go travelling, and in the months before she left Australia, she came back to Burringbar to say goodbye.

Zoe had dislocated her knee dancing and so arrived with a long canvas splint on her leg, held together by thick straps of velcro. Limping around the house with a defiant smile, my sister was restless and jittery.

Our father was angry. Angry that Zoe had given up uni. Angry that she was planning on travelling alone. Angry that he couldn't stop her.

We sat around the kitchen table while my mother prepared dinner. It was my final year in primary school, and I felt myself grown. I wanted to join the adults but didn't quite know how. I was watchful, looking for a way in.

'You can't head overseas with a bung leg!' My father drew on his cigarette. 'What if it doesn't get better?'

'It'll be fine,' Zoe said. 'The doctor said it would take a few weeks. I'm not going for another month.' She looked at him across the table, sipping her adult wine.

'What about money?'

'I've been saving all year in Sydney—I've got enough.'

'Because I'm not financing your holiday, Zoe.'

I could see my mother's lips tighten as she ground the spices.

'Dad, I never asked you to.' Zoe's face reddened. 'I'm going to work when I get there.'

'Doing what?'

'Dave said he'd get me a job once I got to Patmos. He said everyone wants to hire Australians.'

My father's best friend had recently moved to Greece.

'What would Dave know about working? He hasn't had a job in years.'

'Dad, he's your friend.' Zoe tapped at the tabletop, a tense rhythm. 'He said I'd get a job easily.'

'But what about uni?'

'Maybe I'll come back to it.' She curled her fingers into a fist. 'It just wasn't what I thought it would be.'

'It's a bad idea, Zoe. I'd support you through uni like I do Billie, but I'm not paying anything towards this.' My father stubbed out his cigarette.

Zoe's splinted leg stuck out stiffly from her body and she picked absently at the velcro straps. 'I know, Dad. But I'm going anyway. It's what I want.'

'But what about your leg?' My father lit up another cigarette. 'You can't go with a bung leg.'

I sat and listened as the conversation went round and round. My sister smiled across at me, but her eyes were sad. She fiddled with her damaged leg, and every now and again she loosened the velcro straps and rubbed cream into her swollen knee.

The next day my mother took us to the beach. Hobbling down to the water's edge, Zoe signalled for me to follow.

'I'm going to take the splint off so I can get wet. Can you hang on to it for me?'

It was a job, and I was thrilled to take it. Zoe undid the straps and eased out of the canvas. Handing the splint to me, she carefully sat down on the sand and then nudged forward into the white wash, holding her knee straight. The waves slid up the beach, lapping around Zoe's body then sucking back out. She held her knee firmly against the steady pummelling of the water and stared out at the horizon.

I stood behind her, watching, but Zoe didn't look around. Since she'd been back, I had longed for her to somehow acknowledge how much I'd grown. In that moment on the beach, I wanted my sister to turn around and tell me something secret— something adults told each other—but she just stared out at the ocean.

I wandered up the sand, back to my mother and Jake.

'Why's Zoe so quiet?' I asked, still holding the white splint. 'What's going on?'

Jake was digging in the sand. He stopped and peered at our mother's face.

'I don't know, Jess.' My mother lifted a hand to shade her eyes. 'Sometimes it's hard to do what you want to, when other people don't like it.'

'The trip?'

'Dad's been giving her a bit of a hard time.'

I squinted down at my mother in the bright sun. She rarely said anything about my father when he wasn't there.

'Do you think Zoe should go?' I asked in surprise.

'No, no,' my mother sighed. 'I can see why Dad's worried. I just think he's being a little hard on her.'

I waited for her to say more, but she didn't.

'Jess, you better wait down there.' My mum pointed to the shore. 'She won't be able to get up by herself. Jakey, you go and help her too.'

The two of us ran down the shore, our towels flapping in the wind behind us. We waited there for Zoe until finally she turned around, ready to go.

Lifting her brown arms to us, she was like a broken bird spreading its wings. We pulled her gently from the waves, patting her leg dry with our towels. Leaning on Jake for balance, Zoe awkwardly fitted the splint, and I bent down to fix the straps.

'Thanks, Jess,' she said softly. 'You're a real star.'

≈

On the day before she left, Zoe asked me to play a game of canasta.

'This is a proper game, Jess,' she said. 'I'm not going to let you win like when you were little.'

A challenge.

I found the cards and raced up to where Zoe was waiting in the pavilion. I sat down and stretched out my legs. I could feel myself mimicking my sister's movements: rubbing my knee, lifting a hand to smooth back my hair, glancing sideways into the bush as though there was someone important watching.

I had played canasta since before I could properly hold the cards. My mother used to set me up behind a cardboard box so I could lay the cards flat and nobody could see. For me and my mother it was a friendly game; we had always played it for the pleasure of collecting the sets of cards, the canastas. But I understood that this game with my sister was some kind of test. Zoe watched me through narrowed eyes. My fingers jerked nervously as I arranged my cards, sensitive to her every judging glance. I felt my blood pound in my ears. Finally, I chose one to throw out.

'You're not collecting them, are you?' I asked as nonchalantly as I could manage.

'Well, I just might be …' Zoe replied, but she didn't pick it up.

I was getting increasingly nervous.

'Jess, do you remember how mad you used to get when I won this game?' Zoe's voice was light, but her eyes were cold.

'Yeah.' I was ashamed. 'But we never played the way you did. We always played for fun. I wasn't used to playing your way.'

'Playing to win? Playing properly?' Zoe grinned, but I felt in that moment that she wanted me to fail the test.

The game went on.

'It's kind of ... mean to play that way,' I said, my fingers trembling. 'It's just not as ... fun.'

'You were always so spoilt.' She was stony-faced. 'You never learned to lose.'

This was murky territory.

'You've never lost anything, Jess.'

'I lose all the time.' I tried to smile. 'Heaps of the games I lose. Just ask Jake.'

I picked up a card and then discarded it. Zoe looked down at the pack, and then up at my face.

'You've lost this game, Jess,' she said. She laid all her cards out with determined precision. The game was over. My sister had won. The air around us was full of something weighty, but I wasn't sure what.

It was a test, and I didn't want to fail.

'Okay,' I muttered, confused. 'Good game!'

Zoe counted up her score, then glanced across at me. 'Look, Jess, your fingers are shaking.' She pointed at my hands clutching my cards. 'You're still such a baby.'

I blushed. I was failing the test.

'But why?' My voice was pained. The air seemed to press in against my cheeks.

'You can't handle losing. A. Spoilt. Little. Baby.'

Something inside me stretched and snapped. I felt myself throw the cards in my hand, watching in horror as they spun down to the wooden floor.

'You're always so mean!' My eyes filled up, and I bit the sides of my mouth.

'Tantrum!' Zoe laughed. 'Throwing a tantrum.'

I had failed. I covered my eyes in shame.

'Just as I suspected,' Zoe whispered.

The tears came then, spilling from my eyes in fast lines, and I turned and ran—as I had when I was small—the sound of Zoe's laughter following me through the green.

Creeping in later, I happened upon my sister's notebook, abandoned in the kitchen as though it was nothing. I opened it up. Inside was a mishmash of odd lines of poetry, mixed in with an observation here or there. I did not expect any reference to me, being well aware of my general irrelevance. But there I was, in plain sight. Zoe had recorded this snippet: *Jessie won't ever mature until she experiences rejection.* And I wondered, then and there, if she had made rectifying this deficiency a small part of her life's work.

≈

At the airport Zoe stood lopsided, clutching her heavy travel bag. Our father reached out to hug her, holding her tight and then letting go and rubbing her arm.

'Just be careful, okay,' he said, shaking his head. 'Look after yourself.'

'I will, Dad.'

'And call us. Call us when you need us. It's okay to call collect.' My father's eyes were shiny behind his glasses.

'Dad, I'm just going back to Sydney. I'll talk to you again before I go.'

'I know, I know.'

Zoe leaned over to hug my mother, then me and Jake in turn. I clung on hard to my mother's hand, still ashamed by how badly I'd failed Zoe's test, and frightened by the seriousness of this goodbye.

'Write to me, you guys!' she said, tousling Jake's hair. 'And I'll write to you.'

Jake nodded, and I smiled, still cautious.

'I'll send you my address, Jess, when I settle somewhere. Maybe in Greece. Okay?'

'Okay,' I whispered. With a sudden stab of hope, I thought of all the grown-up letters I might write.

Zoe turned, swung her bag over her shoulder and limped through the airport's sliding doors. Waving from the other side of the glass, in a single heartbeat my sister was gone.

≈

In that final quiet year before I started high school, after both my sisters had left home for good, my body started to flare up. One of my nipples swelled as though it was infected, and my mother took me on a rare visit to the doctor.

'Breast buds,' the doctor said calmly, trying not to smile. 'It's quite common for breasts to develop at different speeds.'

It seemed odd that my mother hadn't known that. She had, after all, once grown breasts herself. At school, my new breasts didn't go unnoticed. A girl from my class told me that she could see them through the armhole of my uniform, and a boy informed me that they wiggled when I ran. For so long I'd yearned to be grown up, to be a woman like my sisters, but these changes to my body were unpleasant. Ugly, even. Every month the blood had started rushing down my thighs, and this too felt like a kind of betrayal, marking me out in some way I wasn't ready for.

I could feel my childhood slipping, my body morphing out of my control, and I did what I had always done—I headed for the trees. Climbing the mountain behind my house, I sat in a thicket of camphors and stared down at my homeplace. You couldn't stop time, even if you wanted to. I cupped my growing breasts in the palms of my hands as the leaves above me rustled a little in the wind. Tiny finches flew in bursts all around me. It was soothing there, the creatures around me going about their lives. I let my hands drop, wondering if Billie or Zoe had ever felt like me. Unwieldy and out of whack. When I'd watched their bodies morph, it had only seemed to make them more powerful. I didn't know why it wasn't the same for me.

That evening, my father came in from the garden with a row of hairless, closed-eyed mice cradled in the hollow of his shovel.

'I found these while I was turning the compost,' he said softly. 'I thought you might want them.'

Gathering up the mice with precise, almost-grown fingers, I made them a warm, dry, hot-water-bottled nest. I fed them from a cotton bud dipped in sugared milk, their tiny tongues lapping weakly as I held them in the curve of my palm. They all died, one by one, over a long, drawn-out week, and I wept with each new cold, unbreathing body. I put them—death by death— in a matchbox in the freezer, where they lay frozen side by side, until finally they were all dead and could be buried together.

I had loved each one in its minute, embryonic perfection.

I didn't see it as a premonition. That just because you love something you cannot make it stay.

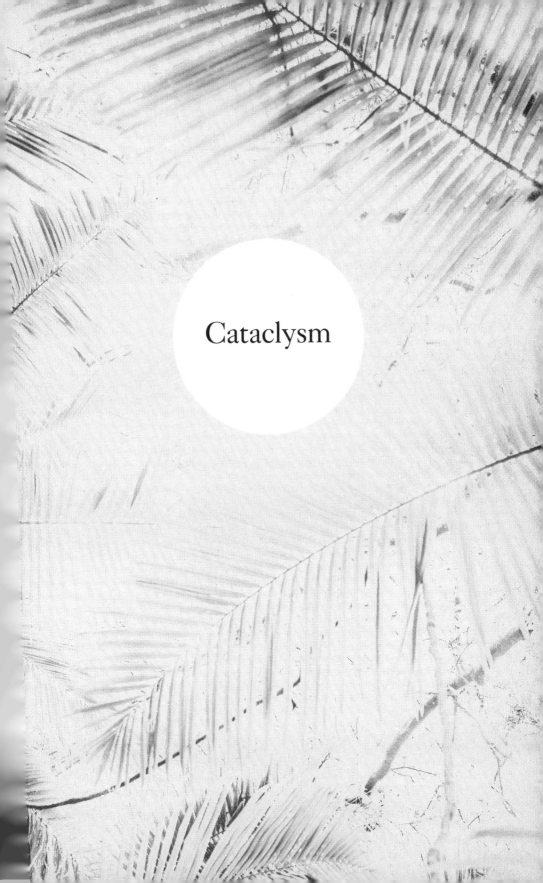

Cataclysm

Two weeks after I started high school, a girl from down the road came over in the afternoon after school. Chatting, teasing and laughing, my friend and I played, until abruptly the girl grabbed my arm and came up close to my face, eyes serious and full.

'Is there something wrong with your mum?'

'No—what do you mean?' I had barely noticed my mother's slow wanderings about the house and garden.

'She just seems really sad. Has something happened?'

The girl's face was so close I could see the light speckling of freckles across her nose. Her long, straight hair swished over my arm.

'She's fine.' I was confident. 'She's always like that.'

Later, the girl bragged at school that she was the first to know. 'I even knew before *her*. My dad told me on the way home.'

When my friend had gone, our mother called us, Jake and me, into the lounge room. Afternoon light swung in through the long glass doors, reflecting off her face. The outside grass was lush and humming with crickets.

'There's something I have to tell you.' Her face was stricken.

I peeked at Jake, saying nothing. Sitting down on the couches, we watched her with startled eyes.

'Zoe's dead. She died yesterday, in Holland.' Her voice was pained, but she didn't cry. She looked at us—ten and twelve—half-grown like awkward, eager puppies.

Jake breathed out in a crumpled, broken laugh.

'She's not *joking*, Jake.' My words were stern, though I had just stifled the same sound, a kind of disbelieving titter, within my own throat.

My mother reached out an arm towards my brother. I could feel my heart banging in my chest. Jumping up, face set, I ran. Into the unbroken green of our land, I ran. I could not cry—could not breathe—and finally, when I felt I might burst, I stopped and my breaths came in sucking gasps. My sister Zoe. Brown-bodied, light-eyed, splint-legged. Songs like swelling rivers. Eyes hard and cold.

'Yes, I'll play, but only if you—Jessie—only if you say, *Zoe is the bestest, most beautiful, kindest, most generous, most amazing sister in the whole world and I love her more than anyone else.*'

But I wouldn't. I just wouldn't. Zoe. Taut-bellied, with a birthmark the shape of Australia on the back of her thigh. All those random moles and freckles. Her skin glimmering beneath my palms. The squeeze of her hand on my shoulder. Her sideways, slant-eyed smile.

'Thanks, Jess—you're a real star.'

I hid then, behind a steep hillock, in the raised roots of a gigantic camphor tree, and waited for someone to come find me.

And my mother came, tentatively calling my name.

'Jess, Jessie ...'

'Mum,' I whispered, my voice dry and scratchy.

'Come on, Jess. You can't stay here.' My mother was still tear-less, her skin stretched tight across her face like a drum.

'How did you find out?'

'The police in Holland rang the police in town, and they rang Dad at work.'

'At work?'

'Yeah. He thought it was one of you kids. A bus crash or something. You know there's been those school bus crashes lately?'

'Yeah, on the news ... Mum, what happened, a car accident? In Holland?'

My mother looked down at the grass. Her hair fell forward and she slowly reached up and tucked it behind her ear.

'Mum?'

'She killed herself.'

'What?'

Tilting her face up, my mother's gaze was unwavering. 'Suicide. The police said suicide.'

'No.' It was impossible. 'Why would she do that? Zoe?'

Shaking her head softly, my mother looked towards the house.

'We'd better go back, Jess. Your dad's coming home from work early and he won't know where we are.'

My father met us in the garden. His skin was grey and he shuffled from foot to foot as though the ground was hot. He wedged his hands roughly into his pockets and then pulled them out again, pushing off his glasses and pressing his fingers against his eyes, his mouth gaping open, a sagging dark hole. Unspeaking, he leaned towards us with outstretched arms, catching us against him in a fierce embrace. My father sobbed, with gasping, tight, dry breaths, and my mother and I stood unmoving in his arms. A wide space seemed to open up between us all and my father squeezed us tighter to try and fill the gap.

Finally my father let go and we drifted, wordless, back inside. In the lounge room we saw Jake was gone. With barely suppressed terror my parents called to him: 'Jake! Jake! Jakey! Where are you, Jakey?'

'Fuck, Janny, where is he? Jake!'

I could see my mother might cry, so deep grew the two lines between her brows.

'Jake! JAKE!'

Immobilised, I watched my parents search the house, all the island rooms. They ran out into the garden calling for him, their voices muffled, wet. 'Jake? Jakey?'

'He's scared, Janny. He's scared to come out.'

My mother found him hiding deep under his bed, tucked up in the corner with the spider webs and dust. Rolling Jake out, my parents brushed him off and scolded him softly through their tears.

'You scared us, darling.'

'Jake, mate, we didn't know where you were.'

As he tried to slip quietly from my parents' grasp, Jake's frightened eyes entreated me, but I could say nothing and do nothing to keep the world at bay. Peering at the ground, away from my family's shock-filled faces, I watched as the heavy tears rolling down my cheeks dropped from my chin and bounced at my feet. My tears seemed to crack the secret roundness that had encircled us—Jake and me—leaving us broken like two halves that could not make a whole.

≈

The day after Zoe died, Jake and I went to school.

'You don't have to go, kids—you can stay home,' my father had said the night before. 'It's just ...' His voice faltered. 'It's meant to be better if you try to do the things you'd normally do.' The psychiatrist in him speaking. 'I'm going back to work, but Mum will be here if you don't want to go to school.'

Keeping up the rituals of normality was decided upon as the best defence against grief, and we got up from bed and ate breakfast at the kitchen table, and then caught the bus from the end of the driveway as we had on every other school day of our lives. I'd left Jake behind at primary school, so it was the first year we weren't catching the same bus. For me, the day was a swimming carnival, and I dressed up in my house colour. In a bright yellow sundress I was a sad-eyed, drooping daffodil. On the bus I watched the faces of the kids around me, wondering if any of them *knew*. No one spoke to me, though they didn't look away either. Finally I turned to the girl behind me, an old acquaintance from primary school.

'My sister died yesterday.' My voice came out a strangled, husky whisper.

'What?' The girl could not decipher my words.

'My sister is dead.'

'Which one?'

'Zoe.'

'You're kidding, right?'

'No.'

My friend looked at me, stunned, uncertain. 'She's been overseas for a while, yeah?'

'Yeah, almost a year.'

'How'd she die?'

'She killed herself. In Holland.'

Silence grew around us and I turned back and faced the front. Trees flicked past the bus window, skidding strips of green. My face felt numb and I reached up and pressed my fingers into my cheeks, hard, until the bones beneath my eyes began to hurt. Tears sprang up—I could taste them, wet and salty, in the back of my throat.

The swimming carnival was loud and echoing. Screaming kids lined the grandstands, pompoms and streamers springing furiously in their arms. I hung back in the very last row of benches, hoping to go undetected among all the cheers, a single thought on repeat in my mind.

This is the first day I will live when Zoe is dead.

A teacher approached me, her hair tied in two messy plaits and laced with yellow ribbon. Her face was set in lines of irritation.

'You're not swimming today?' she asked. 'That's a pretty party dress. Bit much for a swimming carnival, though.'

My mother had made the daffodil dress when I was still a child at primary school, and though it hugged at me now with all my budding curves, I felt *myself* in it. Running my fingers through the pleats in my dress, fanning the yellow fabric out around me, I was comforted. The teacher looked me up and down with disapproving eyes.

'Why aren't you swimming? This isn't a day for being lazy, for just hanging out.'

I said nothing.

'What, you can't talk either? Won't swim, can't talk.'

'My sister's dead.'

'What?'

'My sister died yesterday. She killed herself. In Holland.'

Stepping backwards, the woman looked away, her lips pressed together tightly.

I had transgressed, speaking those words, and as I stared at the part zigzagging down the back of the teacher's hair, I wondered in what way I could possibly speak the words right.

My sister passed away.

My sister passed on.

She took her own life.

She breathed her last.

She departed this life.

I tested these phrases beneath my breath, shaping them with my mouth, trying them out.

Gave out. Expired.
Broke down. Perished.
Suicide. Crashed.

The cheers of the surrounding kids surged around me, and I lifted my hands to cover my ears.

When she turned back to face me, the teacher's mouth had not softened. 'Well, at least try to look as if you're having fun.'

I nodded in cautious reply, dropping my arms to my sides. I didn't know if I should stand or sit. I didn't know if I should speak or keep silent. The whole world was filled with uncertainty. Nothing was clear. I was lost in this new terrain, where Zoe was dead and there were no words to speak right.

On the way home, I stared out the bus window and thought of my mother's face and how it might look. I remembered Jake's imploring eyes from the day before when they'd pulled him out from under the bed. On hearing Zoe was dead, I had run and my brother had hidden, as though the shock had physically propelled us. Animal instinct. I thought about the crease between my mother's brows—how hard it suddenly seemed, frightening instead of reassuring, as though her face was held in a tight mask to keep it from collapsing inwards.

Through the windows, the silhouetted mountains disappeared from sight as the bus neared my driveway. I imagined my father's slapping shoes on the bricks of the walkway as he arrived home from work to find the house so filled with our silence that we could all barely breathe for the sadness.

Again I lifted my hands and cupped them over my ears.

The bus door opened to let me out, a hissing, clanking slide, and I wandered slowly down the driveway, prolonging that awful moment when I would see the loss of my sister reflected back at me in the eyes of those who made up my family.

≈

The next morning, on waking, I lay in bed in a peaceful haze. The birds were noisy outside my windows and I listened, still half-asleep, picking out my favourite sounds. Small moments of ignorance. The realness of the day burst upon me and I rolled out of bed and stood before the mirror. My bed-shirt was a crumpled soft orange, with a large hand-drawn number four, and it hung off one shoulder.

Zoe's old shirt. Her basketball shirt. She was number four.

Smoothing my palm across my sick-feeling belly, I watched my own reflection.

It's in my eyes. Her gone-ness. This is the second day I am alive while Zoe is dead.

I lingered in the bedroom, still afraid of what my parents' faces might look like. Finally, I walked out to the kitchen. I could feel my parents' sorrow slowly filling the house—all the nooks and crannies—everywhere bleak with their loss.

The kitchen was airless, though all the sliding doors were open. My family sat waiting. There were plates of toast already buttered and I sat down at the table. We were having a family meeting. I glanced at my mother's face, but it was unreadable in the morning light.

'Look, kids,' my father began, 'your mum and I, we want you to know that it's okay for you to ask us any questions.' His eyes filled with tears. 'We want you to come to us when you need to talk about it.' He forced down a sob in his throat. 'We don't want you to be afraid to talk about *anything*, okay?'

My mother stayed still and silent. I looked down at my toast and soundlessly pushed my plate away.

My father sighed, his breath uneven, battling on. 'We don't want you to think we can't handle it, because we can.' He took off his glasses and swiped at his eyes, but the tears kept coming.

Neither Jake nor I spoke. My father tried to rally himself.

'So, we don't really know what was happening for Zoe.' He pulled out a cigarette with shaky fingers. 'The police couldn't tell us much.'

I nodded, still staring at my plate.

'I'm collecting up all the letters she sent, getting Dave to send his from Patmos, trying to get a picture.' He flicked at his lighter. 'But the important thing is … we've all got to stick together.'

My father was trying to pull us in close, but all I could feel was the distance between us.

'Okay?' He stood up and stepped towards the sliding glass doors, lighting his cigarette. 'Kids?'

My throat was dry. Gulping, I forced out a 'yeah'. I glanced at Jake, who sat motionless beneath our father's words.

'Okay,' our father repeated, sucking on his cigarette, his face lined and drooping. After a few desperate puffs, he walked away to shower for work.

I peeked up through my lashes at my mother, trying to gauge her emotions behind the tight smoothness of her skin, the strange clearness of her eyes. She was, in that moment, both familiar and unfamiliar—known and unknown—and I was frightened of what I might find searching her face. I could not eat the toast, so I gathered up my schoolbag and walked through the door. Wandering up the driveway, alone among the white pebbles and the overgrown shushing bamboo, the sickness in my belly dissipated, though it did not disappear.

At school a growing whisper whipped around me like a fresh-lit bushfire, and I looked away from all the curious eyes. Words trailed me as I lined up with the others for morning assembly.

'I heard she was raped over there and that's why she did it.'

'That's her little sister, there with the long hair.'

'Her dad's a psychiatrist.'

'She's kinda pretty, don't you think? I like her bangle.'

'Why would her sister kill herself? Something must have happened to her.'

It had only just occurred, but my sister's death seemed already to overshadow me. I had become—quite suddenly—*that girl*.

The sister of the girl who killed herself, you know the one?

And not just in the other kids' eyes, but inside me too. Whoever I had been before was swallowed by the enormity of what Zoe had done. I couldn't have a single thought without it pinging back to her.

Zoe's dead. Zoe's dead. Zoe's dead. Zoe's dead.

Looking down at the speckled cement beneath my shoes, I stood uneasily on a jagged crack that reached away from me like the outstretched branch of a tree. It was only two weeks since I'd started high school but my new black school shoes were already showing signs of wear, the toes chafed to a pale grey and a fine thread poking out along the strap. I fought the urge to bend down and pull at the black thread, to unravel it. The principal's nasal voice droned overhead, his words indistinct and monotone, and after an agonising wait in the morning sun, we were dismissed to our classes. High school was a foreign land, a giant step removed from the green pasture of my primary school. It was only half an hour's drive away, but it seemed so far from home. This new school housed over one thousand students and was a grey fortress, equipped with trapdoors and false rooms and a maze-like sameness. All the local primary schools fed into this one big high school, and in my classes I'd been separated from anyone I knew. My ragtag pack of primary school peers were scattered, and it was hard to find a familiar face.

I felt myself curl inwards as I walked, the weight of my bag heavy on my back. I didn't have an internal map of this ad hoc establishment, and between every lesson, when I moved from classroom to classroom, I was quite often stranded with no idea which direction to go. A Block, B Block, C Block, D Block, the quad, the toilets—all frustratingly intertwining and unrecognisable. I couldn't negotiate the square stairwells and the dull hallways in their uniformity, and was always lost before my first class. Breathing in, I tried to calm my rising pulse, and kept on walking.

I arrived for geography ten minutes late. The teacher's eyes skidded away from my face as I stood in the doorway.

'Jessie, come in. Sit down.'

Sitting on a red plastic chair, I pulled out my folder and pencil case, placing them on the desk before me. This teacher knew Zoe and Billie, had taught them both. Out of place in my rural high school, she had the sad face of a French movie star from the foreign films I watched with my parents, movies where the heroines smoked cigarettes and cried with beautiful mascara-lined eyes. I sought in this teacher a compassionate soul, and watched her carefully for a signal that she understood it was the second day that I was alive and Zoe was dead. Listening as she talked about mountains forming and the recording of rainfall, I waited and waited. Her eyes wandered over me, and something inside me shrank tightly away.

After a minute, I raised my hand.

'Yes, Zoe?'

There was an intake of breath around me, the other kids taking in the teacher's misstep. My cheeks slackened—a kind of involuntary release—as though all life suddenly withdrew from my face.

The teacher blushed under her foundation. 'I'm so sorry, Jessie. That was … an accident. It's just … I always got you and her confused.'

I looked down, away from her sad eyes. Hair falling forward, I hid my face from the other kids' stares.

'Did you have a question, Jessie?'

'No.' I shook my lowered head and my hair fluttered out around me. Frozen by the unexpected mention of Zoe, I could not think what it was I had to say. Hot-cheeked and exposed, I waited for the teacher to begin again her talk of mountains and rainfall. In time, the electronic bell-horn sounded—loud and unforgiving—and we all trooped off to our next class.

On the way, I was lost again, and stood in the hallway a moment trying to get my bearings. From behind I felt a hand suddenly on my shoulder. Another teacher, her face puffy and red, was grasping at my arm. She held a crumpled tissue at her nose. Behind large dark glasses, the woman's eyes were disguised. Her fingers pressed into my skin, but she did not speak. She lifted her glasses from her face with a trembling hand. Tears streamed from her eyes, and she shook her head, wordless and distraught. I was startled, and the path of kids around us curved away from me in an unspeaking line. I felt marked, contagious even, as though the kids feared the sorrow around me was catching.

'Jessie, I can't ... Jessie, I'm so sorry.' The woman's fingers felt suddenly limp, and they dropped away from me. With fumbling hands she replaced her glasses, the tears running down her cheeks beneath the plastic rims. 'I can't believe she's gone, that's all.'

I stared at her and she began to crumble.

'I can't. I can't ...' she kept muttering, then she turned to walk away and disappeared unsteadily down the hall.

Standing at the doorway of my music class, I hesitated,

apprehensive of this particular teacher's forceful manner. She had been Zoe's music teacher and I had once seen her perform a semi-humorous striptease in a school musical I attended as a young child. Dressed all in black for this class, she had a line of light pink lipstick smeared across her thin lips. I waited for her to notice me, to give me some sign she knew Zoe was dead. Prickling with sensitivity, I was pulsing, electric.

The plastic seats were arranged in a vague curve of rows, the desks removed, and as my classmates filtered in they sat down and looked about suspiciously. I sat in the middle row and waited. When everyone was seated, the teacher strode out to the front of the room and looked about, meeting nobody's eyes.

'Today I thought we'd try something different and learn a song. Here are the lyrics. It's the theme song from *MASH*.'

She handed out sheets of paper, still warm from the photocopier.

'I'll play the music on this tape, and you all sing along.'

I looked down at the page and read the first line of the song.

Suicide is painless.

The words rushed at me as though I'd been smacked. On my teacher's face there was no sign of acknowledgment; her eyes skimmed past mine as if I wasn't there and Zoe wasn't dead. Turning the tape on, she glanced about expectantly, and my classmates began to sing. I couldn't shape the words, my mouth numb and heavy. The song was long, with the awful first line repeated as an incessant refrain. When the voices around me wavered, the teacher stopped the tape and rewound it, starting again from the beginning. I felt I had entered some sort of dreamscape, a world that was elongated and slightly askew. It was hard to comprehend that no one else noticed. I wanted to stand up and walk outside, away from the repeating words of the ugly song, but I was stymied, suspended in time.

Halfway down the page, the girl beside me reached out a delicate hand and placed it on my knee.

I jerked towards her.

'Hang in there, Jess,' she whispered, her brown eyes kind. I felt the strangeness of the room subside the smallest fraction. 'She doesn't know about your sister, or she doesn't know that you're her sister. I'll tell her when it's finished, don't you worry about that.'

I smiled then, and my eyes filled with tears that I did not want to shed. The girl smiled back and softly squeezed my leg. When the song was done, I sat stunned, the girl's hand still resting on my knee—one warm skin connection in a world that had become a haze of unbearably shuttered glances. The bell-horn rang again and I stood up to flee.

'Wait for me, Jess. I'm going to tell her.' The girl was angry, her cheeks two bright pink spots.

I stumbled outside, dragging my bag, unsure of what to do, of where to be. I was afraid of the teacher—all dressed in black—afraid of how her eyes had skidded over me, afraid of what they might look like if they stopped and took me in.

It was recess and I stood and waited for my new friend, watching my classmates spill out the door. I could hear nothing from inside and I fought the impulse to bolt. After a few minutes, the girl appeared in the doorway, hot and ruffled, her blonde hair sticking to her forehead.

'I told her,' she said simply, pulling her bag over her shoulder.

'What did she say?'

'She said she *forgot*. Can you believe that? What a cow.'

'Thanks for telling her. It made me feel sick.'

'I know. You were shaking. I heard about your sister. I'm sorry, it must be real sad, hey? How are your mum and dad taking it?'

'They seem all right, but … everything's gone weird. I don't like looking at their faces, and nobody wants to look at mine.'

'No one knows what to say,' she said casually, but she herself didn't seem stuck for words. 'Do you miss her?'

'She'd been overseas for a year. It's hard to tell she's really dead.' It was a relief to finally speak. 'Sometimes I can't remember her face exactly, because she's been gone a while, you know? When I look at a photo I remember, but then later she disappears again. I don't know how to hold her in my mind.'

'Nobody I know has ever died.'

'It all feels wrong.'

'It must be hard. Why'd she do it?'

'I don't know. No one does.'

'You'd think something real bad must have happened to her.'

'Nothing real bad. Well … nothing I know.'

She paused a second, thinking. 'Hey, Jess, you want an icy pole? I'll shout you. Mum gave me a dollar today.'

'Thanks. It's hot, hey?'

93

We strode together towards the canteen and I felt the cloud of isolation that had so completely engulfed me begin to lift. I glanced at the girl beside me, with her doll-like pink cheeks and her dirty blonde hair, and I couldn't help smiling. Stranded in an alien landscape, I was finally found. At the canteen we paused in the shade, two twelve-year-old girls in our striped school uniforms, licking our icy poles and giggling as the melting drops ran down our fingers.

Standing there with her beneath the corrugated-iron roof, I was visible. One small moment of lightness, the sun shining brightly in my eyes.

≈

Billie's body convulsed with sobs in the back seat of the car, her arm shuddering against my shoulder, knocking me in a sad rhythm. Across the sea Zoe was dead, and Billie had taken leave from her city life and come to Burringbar for the weekend. The bush was green and large and it loomed over us, as though it had magnified its girth, the sheer voluminous health of the place a sudden affront to our senses. With Billie there, all the places Zoe had once been seemed to goad us through the car windows.

'It's not like this in the city,' Billie sobbed. She pushed the sleeves of her jumper against her eyes. 'I'm so busy I can go to uni and forget about it for a while.'

Jake and I stared at our sister's crushed mouth. We had never seen Billie cry, and that she should weep so soon, when we had only reached the winding road before our driveway, was somehow unexpected. We sat in the car dazed, unmoving, and watched her, the distress of it unbearable. In the front of the car I heard my father exhale, a ragged sound. My mother shaded her eyes, looking sideways out the window. Billie, loose and trembling, leaned forward to rest her head on her knees, shutting her eyes tight.

What would our sister do when we reached the house?

This gone-ness of Zoe was vast. A tear in the fabric of our family, the tear leaving a gaping hole—bottomless and black—for us all to tumble into. Our indomitable biggest sister's sobs just the beginning.

≈

When Zoe died there was no wake, her death so shocking, so unexpected, as to render it beyond marking.

'I miss her already.' Her mother's voice was lost and weak on the end of the phone. 'I can't believe she's gone.'

Zoe's mother travelled to Holland, seeking answers. Scrambling to know how to cope, my parents decided to continue on with life unchanged. My father did not go to Europe for Zoe's funeral, and at home there was nothing, not even a small ceremony. As kids we didn't question these decisions. Weren't they—as grown-ups—the experts? After a while my father erected a huge and beautiful log in the garden in memory of her, but it remained unmarked and lonely. Unexplained. This monument the only dead thing in a garden so lush and lovely, it was almost indecent.

≈

My parents had never put much effort into policing 'normalcy'. I'd go as far as to say they were both more interested in its opposite. So when it came to examining my sister's behaviour leading up to her suicide, and whether or not it had been within the range of normal, they were at something of a disadvantage. The method my sister had chosen to take her own life left no room for doubt. There was not a hint of the accidental. My parents could not comfort themselves by believing there had been some terrible mistake.

In the months after Zoe died, my father began the impossible task of deciphering *why*. Diligently, he collected every letter, every postcard, every stray birthday note, every fragment of poetry that Zoe had scribbled on the backs of scuffed envelopes. Writing to Dave in Patmos, he asked for copies of Zoe's letters. He collected every scrap of her and he sorted through them all, trying to make sense of the chaotic mixed messages and multi-layered meanings. The letters were full of the places she had travelled through—the Philippines, Pakistan, India, Greece, Italy, Germany and finally Holland. They contained descriptions of the people she'd met and snippets of how she was feeling. They were frank, in the way Zoe had always been,

96

but there was no trace of any suicidal thoughts. From a distance I watched as my father numbered all Zoe's letters in order of when they were received, and then, when nothing became clearer, he numbered them in order of *importance*. Classifying and reclassifying them, he searched for signs, but there was no sense to be made and in the end he found himself tangled and lost.

Zoe's suicide note, found with her body, had not been illuminating. It was messy and angry and muddled. Less an expression of intent than a drunken mishmash of words, roundabout and indistinct. Reading it left my father nauseous and disorientated. The more he looked at Zoe's final scrawled words, the less he understood her, but there were three short lines that hammered at his heart.

Listen to the song for me, Dad.

If you can listen to me.

Listen to me, Dad.

These words wrapped their tendrils about his throat. Rapacious and invasive, they climbed over him, their spiny shoots searching out his mouth and nose and ears, slowly breaking within. Zoe's last words pushed open cracks inside him. In the aftermath of my sister's death, my father could not make sense of her, but he understood that she had felt herself unheard, and by him most of all.

The last letter my family received from Zoe arrived two weeks after she died. My parents hadn't known it was coming. When it arrived they expected it to be an explanation. My father gripped the white envelope with shaking hands, falling into a chair at the kitchen table to read it. But it was just a letter, like all the others, full of life and plans. It ended with the request:

Dad, is it possible for you to continue my health insurance another 6 months?
  I.S.I.S (STA)
  Policy no. 8634324
  Date of issue: 27/7/89
  Issuing office: SYD LEE ST
  Exp. date: 8/1/90

≈

My father had always championed his right to be whoever he was, moment to moment, unashamedly. And when he grieved, it was with the same degree of commitment.

After Zoe died my father was silent, his face flat, and we watched him with care. We waited for small moments of lucidity or brightness. Wary and worried, we waited for the faintest hint of a smile.

'He's depressed,' my mother said after she found me watching him in the study.

'But Mum, will he ever get better?'

She looked off into the distance, out into the garden. 'Everything takes time, Jess. I don't know how long it might take.'

'We just have to wait?'

'Mmm.' My mother nodded, and then wandered outside. She

picked up a fallen palm frond and dragged it to the edge of the bank as I trailed behind her. 'We're all just sad, Jess.' She threw the palm frond over the edge and then searched out another, looking at the ground, not at me. 'We miss her. I don't know what we can do.'

My father's guilt quietened him. He couldn't go on with the garden, his sculpting of the world. The forest that had once held us all so firmly offered him no comfort. He felt no joy in its green embrace. He sat, instead, and read the newspaper, but he did not get past the front page. Grief time was like deep time, geologic— change was imperceptible. On his work days he got up early and left, the ticking minutes an awful weary grind, his patients blur-ring into one large mass of desolation and despair. But the torture of those interminable seconds was nothing compared with being at home and alone with his thoughts. My father could not sleep, food turned to ash on his tongue, and he drank wine like water. His only relief was the haze of drunkenness. We all stepped around him, giving him space in his sorrow, but the gnarled, woody vine of his guilt tightened around his beleaguered heart.

≈

In secret, I too began to search out the mysteries of my sister's sudden end. Squashed into the overfull filing cabinet, in cream manila folders, I found all Zoe's letters home. In unsurveyed moments—out of range of my parents—I crept into the study to investigate their contents. Expecting to find clear indications of deep sorrow, or covert references to drugs and disorder, I was instead confronted by my dead sister's ambiguities, her elusive turn of phrase. Though I read them all, and read them all again, I could not properly understand them.

What did I really know of my sister? So much of how I had seen her was my own childish fantasy of what it was like to be a teenager. As a kid, I'd rarely been able to break through my projection of who Zoe was to see any of her woundedness. The vision I had of her—that punk acrobat, so full of verve—had overshadowed my whole childhood, but it had also stopped me from truly knowing her. After she died, my memories of her felt corrupt, based so heavily on a misconception. The sister I had experienced would not have taken her own life. So who was this vulnerable, desolate girl?

Lying awake, night after night, I tried to imagine Zoe's travelling life, but the names of all the foreign countries got mixed up in my mind and I couldn't sort them out. I closed my eyes and strove to summon my dead sister's face—her slant-eyed smile, her burnished glow—but every day the image blurred further, threatening to dissolve. I fought this forgetting, training my mind to work round and round fragments of memory until slowly they embedded inside me. The things I remembered about Zoe may have been tainted by my childish perspective, but—apart from her letters home—they were all I had. In the hours before sleep I counted these memories like a silent mantra. Working through this invisible rosary beneath the cover of night, I diligently kept track.

Perhaps this was my own type of magical thinking. Perhaps I believed that if I kept Zoe alive in my memory, she wouldn't really be dead. Before she died, she'd been away for a year, immersed in what could only be—for me—a kind of fantasy-scape: the wider world. Perhaps she still existed somewhere in that imaginary place?

≈

You think if someone you love takes their own life, in the end you will find out why. It is a dark mystery that needs solving. But unless they explicitly explain it, the truth is you may never know. We all long for meaning—that elusive cause and effect, a story that makes sense—but resolution of even the most basic questions often relies on guesswork. Hazy, unsure; supposition.

While Zoe was travelling, it was as though she had existed in three parallel spaces. Her exterior real-body-life, where she was interacting with the world at large; the effervescent 'self' of her letters home; and some deeper, unarticulated place where she had wanted to die. It was a terrifying thought. What did my sister not say that we should have intuited? What else about our loved ones were we not intuiting? In hindsight, every interaction was much more significant, strewn with missed clues and undetected signs. And afterwards, everything—every interaction—seemed uncertain, filled with risk.

≈

After my sister died, my parents stopped hosting the wild parties of my childhood. They bought a VCR and hired endless movies, filling the sudden void in their lives with other people's stories. We rarely went out, but sometimes one of them would rally, and we'd head off to a house party somewhere in Burringbar. Whole nights of drunken laughter, guffaws and high-pitched feminine shrieks. As a small child, I hadn't noticed the unhappy faces of the watching women whose husbands so tightly held the writhing bodies of their dancing partners. I'd slept in curled oblivion long before any of the drunken arguments began. It was only after Zoe died, when I was dangling over the abyss of adulthood, that I noticed the horror of all the excess. I saw men fall off verandahs, come up with bleeding foreheads, wipe the blood from their eyes and still down another beer. I saw mothers rage at fathers, incessant and frightening, their eyes hard and wounded, their words slurred. Jake and I moved aside when stray couples wanted to use a room for a quick fumbled fuck.

'It's been a while, kids. You know what it's like.'

All these things came irrevocably sliding into view, and the parties felt suddenly filled with a hollow kind of cheer. The hopeful sound of my childhood gave way to a cacophony of dark and drunken despair.

Zoe was dead, and the grown-ups no longer seemed grown up.

Grief has its own time line. While other people's lives moved forward, ours were stuck at this one harrowing point. A lot of things can happen in a year, but a grieving-year can feel like no time at all. As a family, we couldn't move on. Zoe's death still felt like yesterday. The pain didn't lessen. My father didn't start to smile. Gradually my parents fell away from the community they'd helped build. Maybe there wasn't room for their sorrow, or a place outside the party to talk of what they'd lost. Or maybe there weren't the necessary words. After a time, people we'd once been close to slipped out of sight. It was hard to know if we'd become hermits or if the town itself had begun to look away. But where once my life had been filled with other adults, after my sister's death they mostly seemed to disappear.

≈

My father had always been a social drinker, but after Zoe died his drinking changed. He began to drink alone. Halfway through his first bottle of wine my father's face started to transform. His skin reddened and his eyebrows protruded. His eyes behind round glasses became milkier and his cheeks more jowly. His voice turned harsh and soon it would *begin*. My father talked and talked, an angry monologue of grief, until one after the other Jake and I got up from the table and quietly left. It was as though our father had become infected by rage, and he couldn't shake it. My brother and I found refuge in television or hanging out in our now separate rooms, but our mother stayed and listened. She did not argue, she did not inflame, but sat unbending and calm beneath our father's lashing words.

Jake and I went to bed to avoid his incessant ranting, but my room was closest, and I could hear my father as I lay listening in the dark. The menace in his voice carried through the air. I could hear him threaten my mother, and I listened in terror for a silence so ominous and deep that I could not mistake its meaning. I waited and waited for the sound of my mother's footsteps on the walkway bricks, so I would know she had escaped to bed, and then I waited—my whole body alive with dread—to see if my father's heavy footsteps would follow. I was panic-stricken about what I would not hear once my father had her alone in their bedroom, and the ringing of this waiting silence filled my mind until I could think of nothing but *the plan*.

In the plan I would know the moment when I needed to act. The sound of the silence would tell me, or perhaps a noise, a frightening, meaningful noise, and I would creep from my room. Sliding across the back garden in the dark, I'd slip in through my brother's half-opened door and wake him. Jake would be disorientated with sleep and fear and he'd stumble out the door behind me. I would drag him through the jungle palms, and then, when I thought we were far enough from the grief-rage of our father, I'd urge him into a run and we'd race out towards the ridge and slide down the muddy slope to the secret place of our childhood in the cold, hard darkness.

Our clothes would tear against the barbed wire and we'd graze our backs trying to slide beneath its jagged edge, but once we made it to our secret place we would not stop running. We would race along the creek, our feet slamming against the sharp edges of the rocks. Blinded by the night, Jake and I would run and run until we were free of my father, then we'd huddle together, wretched and shivering under the dark trees, knowing that in our panic we had left our mother behind. We had left her to defend herself against our thrashing, drowning father.

In my escape plan I could not rescue us all.

But most nights my father didn't follow my mother to bed. He stayed up late instead, drinking more wine and playing old records so loudly I couldn't sleep. He listened to the first few bars of Judy Garland singing 'Somewhere Over the Rainbow', just the first line, over and over, as though in his drunken sorrow he was trying to capture the one epic moment when the music swells and she begins to sing. Zoe was gone, vanished from our lives, but to my father this one phrase of notes was like holding in his palm the smallest particle of her. Every night he listened to this first line, as though grasping in his hand the skirts of the girl who had left him, as though in these soaring seconds he could keep her in the room. And when the line was over, she had escaped his hold, and his grief returned in a colossal swamping wave.

And then he played it again.

And again.

My father was stuck in a circular grief and it played upon his mind like the repeating record scratched against my heart.

I listened with a fury so immense I felt it rock and surge inside me, and sometimes when my anger overrode my fear I stormed out of my bedroom to confront him. 'Dad, we can't sleep. Do you not understand that we have to go to school tomorrow?'

My father stood unsteadily in the doorway, unable to hear me over the amplified orchestral strings.

I shouted then, my whole body shaking. 'Turn. It. Down.'

He shuffled to the record-player and turned the volume down a tiny notch, and I shook my head, holding my body stiff in defiance.

'It's still too loud,' I hissed.

His anger roused, my father exploded. 'It's my fucking house! I can do what I want in my fucking house. You've all gone off to bed and I'm just listening to some songs, my favourite songs, you know? Me! I can't do anything in this fucking house without you all fucking complaining.'

He stood over me, radiating a pulsing, drunken violence. I could not let go of my closed fists. I took a sharp breath, my body still trembling.

'Dad, I have a test tomorrow and I need to sleep.' My words came out in a dull monotone. I couldn't bear the necessity of speaking them. 'The music is driving me insane.'

Why didn't he know we needed to sleep? This man who had once been so tender. I wanted to wail but I could only stand before him and speak my muted words. We were deadlocked, and neither of us could win. I turned from him then, blood pounding at my temples like the flapping of wings. I went back to bed and lay awake the night through, listening to the relentless welling of my father's one sad song. I could not cry, though I longed more than anything to feel the hot, slipping release of tears.

In the mornings, my father pottered about as though the night of rage and Judy Garland had never happened. He made a point of telling me daily, 'I love you, Jess. Never forget. I love you.' Once Zoe was gone my father repeated that sentence to me like a chant, and I squirmed and shuddered at his desperate tone. Horribly, blatantly, these words were juxtaposed against his nightly rants and violent, grief-filled rages.

I looked to the gone-ness of Zoe, at the great lack, my sister's shadow, and whispered, 'Here it is. Is this what you wanted? This dark love? All the focus on you?'

In disarray my father swam upstream, enraged and exposed, manic and sorrowful. Drowning. His words insistent and choked with tears. 'I love you. I love you. I love you. I'm sorry.'

As he floundered, I hovered nervously at the edges of rooms. I couldn't bear the endless spilling words and the constant swill of wine. I kept moving, and when I finally went to bed I felt the movement frantic inside me. In my bed I lay motionless but I could not slow down my speeding, pounding heart.

≈

In the year after Zoe's death, the father we had known slowly disappeared, the weight of his grief leaving him misshapen and unfamiliar, until we faced a stranger who was both irrational and unkind. Jake and I—now half-grown—slid in and out of our father's company with averted eyes and frozen faces, tightly wound and trembling.

In the midst of our father's grief-rage the notes of Jake's guitar sounded, unplugged and plinking. He lay on the couch, snuggled deep beneath a doona, endlessly watching quiet television and clutching his guitar. He made himself small and our father's enraged gaze skipped over him, unseeing. Sometimes I lay with him on the couch—slipping in close beside him, trying to breach the silent space that now lay between us.

I'm sorry, I wanted to whisper. *I'm sorry I can't save you from this.*

I couldn't bear to translate all my brother's potent sadness, to speak it out loud, though I felt it mirrored starkly within myself, and a quietness grew about us both, enveloping us until there was no place left for words. Our only communion became a kind of being together, a sitting in the same room. Jake and I exchanged darting glances, but I stopped confirming what was being said. In the wake of my sudden muteness there were only the twanging, lonely chords of his guitar. I didn't tell Jake of my escape plan, nor confess that I lay awake fearing I wouldn't be able to rescue him. I couldn't tell my brother that of everything in my world he was most treasured, most worth protecting, and as the sound of our father's grief-songs filled the house, my silence stretched unchecked between us.

≈

The usual adolescent trials and tribulations that would once have been important to me were difficult to relate to in the context of my sister's death. I found it hard to care what Liz said about Kelly behind her back, or what Justine was wearing, or if Emma didn't get invited to that party of Jack's. All the friends I'd had in primary school, those sibling-like pals, seemed to have drifted away. I tried to keep up with the concerns of my peers, but the enormity of what was happening at home was overwhelming. Even the morphing of my body, which had been so alarming, dimmed in significance. After Zoe died, I didn't know how to be out in the world. Was my every word supposed to reflect—in some subtle way—the pain of what had gone on? Was I allowed to smile? I felt intensely surveyed. Was I grieving right? My classmates were friendly, but I felt like an outcast.

The sister of the girl who killed herself—you know the one?

To escape my dead sister's shadow, in my second year of high school I moved from the cement labyrinth of my overpopulated first school to a smaller school on the hill outside of town. At this new institution I wasn't defined by the suicide of my sister; the students and teachers knew nothing of her story. Starting afresh among reforming delinquents and the devoutly religious, I attempted to reinvent myself as unhindered by my family's engulfing grief.

When Gabriel, the new boy, arrived—black-haired and shining—he walked a clear path towards me and told me his name: 'Gabriel. Everyone calls me Saba.'

'Why's that?'

'Gabriela Sabatini.' A slight roll of the eyes. 'That tennis player.'

I knew of her vaguely.

'Right.'

'But you can call me Gabe.'

In hardly any time at all, Gabe and I slid into a relationship. Looking back, it's hard to fathom just what it was that made us so definite about each other right from the start. For my part, I think I sensed in Gabe a solidity, a steadfastness. I trusted him not to disappear or to suddenly transform. And he was all lightness, bright smiles and big hugs. Endlessly buoyant, always laughing. When I think of myself at this age, and what I might have offered Gabe with all my sadness and confusion, it's tricky to ascertain. But he chose me, and stuck stubbornly to that choice. We were just kids, fourteen and fifteen, but that didn't seem to matter.

Driving to school, my mother asked me if I was thinking about having sex.

'We're already way past that,' I replied, cheeks hot.

I'd grown up surrounded by casually conducted sex, so it was no surprise I wafted into it so easily. Between Gabe and me, there'd been no discussion, only a sudden jump from kissing to more. We were two hippie-kids who'd never been told it was wrong. My parents researched the best contraceptive pill, and upgraded my single bed to a double. No one batted an eyelid. My mother walked in on us once, Gabe's head tucked neatly between my thighs, my breaths shuddery and fast. Her face, usually so still, lit up with surprise. No doubt we were all startled, but before my mother closed my bedroom door I saw a look of elation cross her face. *At least*, I imagined her thinking, *at least they were trying that out.*

Gabe and I moved schools again together—another large,

rambling affair with more options and less surveillance. When we'd first gotten together I'd believed he'd be just 'a boyfriend' in a string of boyfriends. Wasn't I a teenager? Isn't this what we did? But our relationship continued, and I realised with surprise that I would not kiss lots of boys. I didn't even know any other boys, though I passed them daily in the corridors and classrooms. Gabe and I existed on an island, just us two. Unshifting and solid in the tumultuous sea of teenage heartbreak, in time we became young creatures of habit, quiet in our certainty and our everyday routines.

Our closeness made me feel safe, but it could sometimes be stifling, and I began to search the horizon for some other signs of life. I found it in the friendship of the girls in my classes. I'd always been casual about schoolwork, but when I found these brainy girls, school became a place of poetry and thinking, of discussion and philosophising. These shiny-shiny girls talked and talked and laughed and laughed and fought and fought, and I could be among them and then swim back to be with Gabe, sated and fulfilled.

≈

But at home my father's darkness seeped inside me, the nightly rants and drunken menace leaving a repository of black anger. Small capsules of adrenaline pumped through my veins and burst, infinitesimal explosions that left me shaky and filled with fear. I navigated between three worlds: school, the island of me and Gabe, and the murky waves engulfing my green garden home. Sometimes I found myself lost in treacherous waters and was shipwrecked somewhere unexpected.

One day in class we had to write a short story, and I wrote about my dad and his sad eyes disappearing from me down a tunnel of incomprehension and despair. I wrote about his familiar, soothing palms with their dry, soft skin that no longer reached out to squeeze my arm, and I lost my moorings.

When the bell rang I stood up, unable to stop my tears, and collapsed in a shocked slump against the wall, my classmates' eyes flitting away from me in fright. I spoke then—a monologue of hurt and shame and fury—and the teacher whisked me off to the staffroom for a *rest* and *cup of tea*. They called Gabe from his class to be with me, and he came and wrapped me in his easy embrace.

On the weekends I'd stay with my bright-eyed classmates and we drank, the rest of them a little tipsy but me racing recklessly towards the blackness I could sense within. In the morning I'd wake up sick, trembling with dread over where I was and what I'd done. The empty space where Zoe had been haunted me, reminding me of all that I was not. The beach days with my sisters—their shimmering beauty—hung in the back of my mind, leaving me disappointed and forlorn. I was not hard-bodied and sleek, but small and soft and curved. I neither cartwheeled, skateboarded, danced nor sang. I was not ferocious nor dazzling, but quiet, with downcast lashes and blushing cheeks. I looked to the space where my sister had been and a great emptiness echoed back at me. Large and deep, this stark lack settled into the hollow where all my childhood dreams had lain.

And ever so slowly Zoe—the actual person—disappeared from our lives, drifting around in the depths of withered memories until she became an *event*, instead of a person. I clasped my hands tightly around the string of invisible rosary beads—my memories—but even the photographs of her began, over time, to fade, pushing her further from the reaches of recollection. And every year, as the person gradually diminished, the event of Zoe's death expanded. The event lived on—her suicide—breaking away at each of us, pulling us to pieces.

≈

Four years after Zoe died, my father's grief turned wild and the tangled threads of his control snagged and tore apart. Zoe's scrawled letters had finally dismantled him, the rampant vine of his guilt growing noxious and strangling. Evading sleep, his night-time monologue of grief burst into the day. We woke to find he had partitioned off the kitchen with an ad hoc wooden screen to which he'd nailed all his favourite books. The kitchen table was piled up with books that hadn't made the cut. He'd erected a shrine in our kitchen, to Zoe and to all his squally grief.

'Kids, kids. Look, what do you think? Fucking great, hey?'

I slid towards the door, watching Jake as he tried to sit down at the book-laden table.

'I'm not sure about the John Cowper Powys. Your mum's always hated that book. Boring, she says. Fucking boring. Janny?'

My mother stood beside the toaster, waiting for the toast to pop up. Holding her morning sarong in place, she tried not to look at the newly constructed shrine.

'Jess, what about you? You haven't read any Kafka. You've got to, baby! I've nailed this one up here. All these books, they're between me and her. All for Zoe. She'll know. She'll know, even if you guys fucking don't. Janny, don't tell me Kafka's fucking boring! Kids, your mum actually does like Kafka, even if she's not willing to admit it. Tell them, Janny! Fucking Zoe will know. So what do you guys think? How do you like it? The end of the hammer broke off last night, otherwise I'd add those ones too. Some Mishima ... *The Leopard*.'

My father held the broken hammer in his hand, swinging it from side to side.

'You've taken up half the kitchen.' My mother's voice quavered as she placed a plate of toast in front of Jake. 'There isn't enough space to sit.'

'What? What are you fucking talking about? There's plenty of fucking room to sit. Just move those books over and sit down. You have to complain about everything. God, kids, your mother is such a fucking complainer.'

I crept towards the table and slipped into a chair beside my brother. There was meaning in it somewhere, this literary crucifixion, but Jake and I were frightened. We huddled together over breakfast while my father commenced his ranting early.

'I scattered the ashes last night, out in the garden. It was fucking great, just me and her. I could feel her, Janny. She was with me.'

'You scattered Zoe's ashes? Where?'

'Out there in the garden. It's the right spot. You'll love it.'

My mother tightened her sarong, her lips pressed together in a line.

'Oh, what, you have a problem with that too?' My father's face was red, his jaw jutting forward.

'What about us?' she asked. 'What about Zoe's mother? You didn't ask her. She brought the ashes back from Holland. You can't do things like that without talking about it.'

'Fuck! She's my fucking daughter. I know where she should be. You're such a control freak. You want to control every fucking thing. Well, I'm a free man, Janny.' This was his most frequent night-time phrase, replaying again in the morning. 'You don't appreciate anything I do. You don't like my fucking books, you don't like my fucking kitchen, you wish I'd just fucking shut up, don't you?'

'You're not the only one who's hurting,' my mother whispered.

'The kids, the kids, the fucking kids! All right. Fuck. But I'm not taking the fucking books down. Zoe knows. She knows what it's all about.'

'You can't do this. It's crazy.' My mother's voice was quiet.

'What, now I'm fucking *crazy*? Oh, that's just fucking typical.'

Escaping out to the garden, I gathered some of the grey dust back up. My sister's ashes. I hid them in a painted wooden box

among my jewellery, and—avoiding the kitchen—slipped out to
the driveway and the hissing school bus.

≈

Always a punctual man, my father began to run late for work, and
in the office he made phone call after phone call until his frightened patients, milling about in the waiting room, got up and
went home. He bought a tiny ramshackle house in Burringbar
from friends, on impulse, with a cheque that he wrote out at three
o'clock in the morning, drunk, and he didn't tell my mother. He
dreamed of building an elaborate marble-floored Italian restaurant in his tiny new house, and he drew up designs and called
the architects. He called the bank manager and the builders. He
called old friends and acquaintances.

His secretary phoned my mother, her voice low and disturbed.
'Janny, I'm worried about him. He looks terrible, like he hasn't
slept in days. I can't get him off the phone.'

In the afternoon my father rang to say he'd be home soon, but
he didn't arrive. My mother was frantic, her long skirts twitching
as she paced about, the crease between her brows a savage line.
She thought of accidents and car wrecks, and he did not phone
and he did not phone. He vanished, and it took my mother all
the next day—ringing every friend they had—to track him
down. In Brisbane, he'd turned up unannounced on a bewildered
friend's doorstep, clutching a bottle of wine. In the city's giant
shopping centres he'd spent and spent, until his credit cards were
heavy with debt.

'My daughter, everyone thinks she's dead. But she's not—she's come back!' he'd told a stunned woman at a supermarket check-out. 'She was just on holiday. A protracted holiday!'

He took ten hours to complete the two-hour drive home, stopping along the way to make more purchases. He bought a cane furniture suite, a brand spanking new leather lounge, and more and more presents for us, which he claimed post-acquisition were all tax deductible and therefore half price.

When finally he arrived home he still didn't tell my mother about the house he had purchased or the hefty house-sized cheque. He hid the chequebooks, and in the days that followed she couldn't do the banking. Erratic and wired, my father talked and talked, flooding with words. My mother rang his old doctor friends for help and advice.

'He doesn't sleep. He doesn't eat. I think he's having some sort of episode.'

'He's just starting to feel better.'

'No, he's acting crazy. It's beyond that.'

'I saw him the other day at Jim's. He was in high spirits. Life of the party. Back to his old self.'

'No, this isn't normal. He's out of control.'

The next morning, my father's day off, a handyman came to spray the orchard with white oil, but my father made him sit down and watch music videos.

'See how when Clapton comes on stage, Neil Young shifts over? They can't stand each other. You can see by the way Clapton holds his head. I've got it figured, man. You can see it, right?'

'Well, I don't know … but I guess I should get to work.'

'No, no, man. Just watch this bit. It's fucking great. You can see that Dylan doesn't even want Willie Nelson there. I mean, it's Dylan's concert, right? I can tell just from this one look. There, that bit, did you catch it? See how Dylan kind of smiles right there? Here, I'll rewind it for you.'

He had developed detailed theories about what the videos *meant*, and he sat and stood and sat and stood and talked to the handyman until finally it was late and the bemused man escaped into the night.

The next week my father's oldest friends rang my mother with concerns—crazy letters and midnight phone calls. He came home late from the office, arms gesticulating with a frenzied flourish, and declared he had something amazing to tell her. First, though, he had to make a few phone calls. My mother waited while he made call after call, until, exhausted and bewildered, she gave up and went to bed. The next morning, a Saturday, he had converted to astrology. Accosting me at breakfast, he dragged me up to the pavilion, then sat across from me with a notepad, asking nonstop questions about my friends and their star signs and jotting down my replies.

I was surprised by this latest obsession, but I sat with him and talked and talked. It felt like the first time my father had heard me speak since Zoe died. He was vibrant, energetic, his arms sweeping out in lavish emphasis. Tentatively, I smiled. I could see my mother watching us from the walkway down below. Leaving to pick up Jake from a friend's house, she lingered a while, unsure, before she walked out to the car.

When my mother was gone, my father stood up and smacked his pen against his page.

'Thanks, Jess—you've told me everything I need to know. I'm working on something special here.'

'Right, okay.' I was confused.

'I'll be back later to tell you what I've found.'

My father went away to his room and when he returned an hour later he cornered me in the kitchen.

'I've discovered something amazing, Jess. Zoe didn't leave me. She didn't fucking leave me. I've got this patient, a fucking beautiful girl—you'd love her, Jess. You'll meet her soon. She's fourteen, and I know that she's really Zoe. She's Zoe reincarnated.'

Standing over me, my father began to cry, a deep collapsing sob.

'She's not dead, Jess. I knew she'd never leave me. I worked it out from all the things you told me, from what you said about the star signs.' He wiped his tears from his cheeks with the heels of his palms.

'But Dad, she's fourteen—how could she be Zoe? She was born way before Zoe died.'

'It's partial reincarnation—one of my patients told me about it. This guy knows about heaps of fucking stuff, baby. I've done a lot of talking with him. Lots of fucking talking.'

'Dad, that's crazy.'

'You don't believe me?'

'No. You're acting crazy.'

I longed for my mother to return and rescue me.

'You want to know something else?'

'No.'

'See this picture?'

My father held up a *Time* magazine with a picture of a black-skinned man with glasses on the cover.

'Do you know who this is?'

'No.'

'It's Arthur Ashe.'

'Who?'

'Arthur Ashe—he's a tennis player who died of AIDS a few years back.'

'So?'

'Do you see anything unusual about this photo?'

'No.'

'That's me. I'm Arthur Ashe. I can tell by the shape of the glasses.'

'But he only died a few years ago, right? Come on, Dad, how's that possible? Who were you before he died?'

'I'm me, baby, but it's partial, you know?'

I fought tears, wanting to be away from him. 'Dad, you've lost the plot. You've totally lost the plot.'

'Fuck, you sound just like your fucking mother! Both of you so fucking critical.'

Escaping to my room, I waited for my mother to come home. Restless and afraid, I locked my door and stood inside watching the green wilderness through the glass. All the trees of my childhood were still there, solid as they'd ever been, but I couldn't feel the comfort of them. I bit the sides of my cheeks, hard, but there was nothing. No pain. I was feeling less and less.

My mother arrived home at the same time as the furniture van, and the delivery man began to unload the lounge suite. My father asked him to stay for dinner and then regaled him with details of his newly acquired astrological knowledge. After dinner he invited the man to stay the night, and then—in a flurry of movement—headed out to a party at a friend's house. We watched him go, exhaling in a communal sigh of relief. This friend was a psychiatrist and a colleague, and surely something would be done. Talking shyly to the bamboozled furniture delivery man, my mother showed him to the spare room.

Late that night the mother of the fourteen-year-old patient rang to speak to my mother.

'Look, I'm worried about your husband. He came to my house—he just dropped by. He says he thinks Zoe has returned. He says he thinks my daughter is her, that she's come back to him. I think he's becoming obsessed with her. He sounds crazy. I don't think it's right—I mean, he's her doctor. It's not safe. He says he wants to take her away somewhere. She's just a kid, you know?'

My mother didn't know what to say, the woman's words slamming against her, leaving her dry-mouthed and afraid. After she hung up the phone she searched and searched, until finally she found the chequebook and the house-sized cheque.

≈

I escaped the quiet fear of the house to spend the night with the shiny-shiny girls. In their bright company I drank and drank, aiming for that swamping blackness. The girls found me crouched in the garden, shivering and wordless, and tenderly they pushed my hair from my face. Bundling me up, they took me to bed. I lay in the darkness, my head pounding and my stomach raw, and eventually I slipped off into a welcome unconsciousness.

In the morning someone woke me to come to the phone. My mother had called and it was urgent.

'Jess?'

'Yeah, Mum—what's wrong?'

My throat felt razored, my voice shrill.

'Jess, it's your dad. He went missing. They lost him at the party.'

'What?'

'He disappeared and they couldn't find him.'

'Where is he? What happened?'

My head was throbbing, and I pushed my fingers hard against my temples.

'He's at the police station,' my mother said. 'The police picked him up.'

I was afraid to speak, afraid to find out why. The silence stretched between us.

'Jess?'

'What did he do?'

'Are you okay?'

'Yeah, I'm all right. Tell me.'

'He broke into someone's house—there was no one home— and put some music on. He turned it up really loud and the police came. He was naked and muddy—he'd smeared himself with something.'

'Is he okay? I mean, is he hurt?'

'I think he cut himself a bit with the glass. You know, from the window when he broke in. But it's not serious.'

'Mum, what's going to happen?'

'He's not going to be charged, I don't think. It was clear that he's not well. They're taking him to the Richmond Clinic.'

'The Richmond Clinic? Where all his patients go?'

'Yeah.'

The phone shook in my hand. I clenched my teeth together until they scraped loudly in my ears.

'I have to go over and bring him some stuff, some books and pyjamas. I can't pick you up. Can you stay there today?'

'Yeah, that's fine, Mum. Is Jake okay?'

'He's quiet, you know—he's worried, I think.' My mother sounded tired and tight. 'Jess, I'll ring you when I get back, okay?'

'Yeah, all right.'

I hung up, and turned around to face the wary eyes of my friends. Shipwrecked, I felt myself slide down the wall to the floor. I looked up at the girls and then stumbled up and outside to retch into the garden. They ran me a bath, and I climbed naked into the warm water, my whole body shaking and numb. The shiny-shiny girls let me soak, poking their heads carefully around the door now and then to check on me. I thought of my father in hospital pyjamas and felt the relentless quickening of that frantic movement within.

$$\approx$$

When my father broke into the strangers' house he carved mandalas into his palms with the glass from a shattered mirror, smeared himself with sewage and ate a packet of cigarettes. His control had unravelled and he was wild and savage and lost. Grief and guilt had overtaken him and he had driven himself from the road. The darkness that engulfed us all in the green garden sea had finally spilled into his outside life in a torrent of mad despair. He was hospitalised, but he soon came out, and then he was hospitalised again. He talked of axes and Aphrodite and splitting skulls, and his old doctor friends called from Sydney and whispered to my mother down the end of the line, 'Do you have any guns there? Get rid of the axes. Get rid of anything weapon-like.'

Then, when the raving was over and the subdued sadness returned, it was somehow *our fault* and he could not forgive us. He was bitter and angry and uncomprehending, and we could not forgive him. He began to speak of my mother as *that woman*, and when she left the house for any reason she would return to the roaring sound of a chainsaw as he chopped down another of her beloved trees.

≈

We fled the house when I was seventeen, in my final year of school. Battle-scarred and weary, my mother rented a tiny yellow cottage by the ocean. The losses were compounding. Zoe, our community, the father we had known, and then—the final blow—our home.

With the disintegration of my family I held on to Gabe like a lifebuoy, shivering and afraid. A year older than me, he had already finished school. Working casually at his parents' small business, he would often come and go. He was always warm and welcoming and when I retreated into his arms taut with anger, fear or sorrow, he wrapped me up tightly and then made me a snack. Whipping up gourmet toast, Gabe fed it to me morsel by morsel until I was revived. Through all the chaos, he joked and smiled, jollying us along. Perhaps I was the ballast and he was the helium balloon. He stopped me sinking beneath the waves and I stopped him—with all his lightness—from just floating away.

The new house was fresh and clean and salty, and at first we found its brightness blinding, so used were we to the forest green. I was off-kilter in the sudden smallness of this strange world— bangs and scrapes and knocked knees at every turn. I had lived my entire life in the caress of a sprawling forest, and the tight proportions of this cottage left me disorientated. In just turning about I bumped into the doorway, or the table or even the wall. I could not adjust to the toning down of movement. Finally free from the writhing of my father's grief, I was black and blue, as though all the bruised imprints I had gathered beneath my skin through the dark years were surfacing like delayed signals of distress.

Jake and I had left our two cats behind when we fled the house with our mother. It's difficult to suddenly relocate a whole menagerie, and we were frightened our ancient cats would not readjust to life elsewhere. A few days later my father tracked us down.

'You take everything and leave me with the fucking cats?' he yelled down the phone.

Enraged, he made a mound to burn all the things we'd left behind: school exercise books, ragged T-shirts, our mother's basket of furry knitting wool, a dusty pile of *New Internationalist* magazines that he had always despised. When it wouldn't light he swore and stamped across the orchard to find the kerosene. Tipping the pungent liquid on the pile, he leaned down and struck a match. The fire exploded in his face, burning all the way up his outstretched arm and across his livid cheeks.

When my mother didn't return to pick up the cats, old and finicky creatures, my father taped them inside a cardboard box and took them down to the waterhole. He'd thought to drown them like kittens, but the box wouldn't sink and the cats clawed their way out. All his plans rebounding, my father waded in and drowned Jake's cat by hand. It fought him with a dying viciousness, but my cat escaped and swam away, then hid in the lantana. After he had drowned my brother's cat, my father crawled up the bank and retched, then stumbled up the forest steps to ring us and tell us what he'd done. I stood stunned on the other end of the phone line, and hung up without a word.

The next day, my father dropped my cat at our new house by the sea, and it raced inside and sat on the kitchen table, frenetically licking its paws with a quiet kind of madness. My father didn't come inside but stood on the doorstep and yelled. His burned skin was peeling, hanging from him in long strips and flapping in the breeze. He pointed at the crimson scratches the length of his forearm, where Jake's cat had fought him from beneath the water. I couldn't look at him, and fled beneath my bedcovers, hands pressed tightly over my ears.

A few days later I received a letter from him in the post.

Dear Jessie,

SOCIETY AND CULTURE EXAM

Question 1
(multiple choice)

Re: CATS
Supposing you lived at Gulargambone, 300 kms from the nearest vet at Dubbo, and your special 12 year old cat was ill i.e. started vomiting nearly every night, and losing hair, and shitting in the corners of the house, what would you do.

(Circle one answer)

1. *Put up with it.*

2. *Drive 20 kms and let it go feral.*

3. *Hit it on the head with an axe.*

4. *Get your neighbour's wild dog to tear it apart.*

5. *Drown it in dam.*

(Remember, this question's worth 5%)

6. *Drive 300 kms to vet for treatment or euthanasia (remember, a 12 year old cat = 90 year old human).*

7. *Put poison in its food.*

8. *Spray it with deadly poison.*

9. *Nurse it until it dies. (Slowly)*

(Assumption is you have no gun)

10. *Give it extra special care by taking it to bed and letting it vomit in your bed instead of the lounge.*

11. *Give it to a friendly neighbour, or your children who love cats, and would love to nurse a dying cat.*

Question 2
(10 marks)

1. *Do the Chinese eat cats and tortoises, and if so, is there a difference between this practice and Australians eating lambs, calves, rabbits, crabs, lobsters, fish or kangaroos?*

2. *Have you ever seen a baby lamb?*

3. *Why were the Japanese so small in size for so long?*

Dad xx

(Good luck in your exam)

I read the letter and then put it in a box at the back of my wardrobe, hoping against hope to forget it, while my crazy-eyed cat went on endlessly licking its paws. This cat lived seven more years—five more than my father. Rickety and strange, there was something frightening and familiar in its maddened gaze.

≈

Without us, the house in Burringbar was grey and dull. Once the mania blew over, my father sagged with sadness and despair, all the fury of his grief becoming muted with his new aloneness. We had begun again in a world of blinding brightness—sand, sun and fresh white light—and he had begun again in darkness, and the rain came belting down.

When my father could no longer bear being home, he arrived at our cottage steps and knocked gingerly on our door. I opened it, knowing it was him, and he stood in the doorway with a shattered smile, a bottle of wine tucked under his arm.

'Jess …' My name slipped from his mouth like a sigh. 'Where's Mum?'

I stared at him, my eyes hard, knowing that he was brokenhearted, but wanting him gone, for this was our new house, and hadn't he—in all his mad rage—driven us from our home? My body tightened, the angry coil within me twisting until I felt it might snap.

But I let him in—I always let him in.

My brother and I slunk around the cottage, silent and disturbed, while our calm mother comforted our broken father. His sadness seemed to expand, filling the cramped lounge room. We held our breath while our father drank wine. We watched the bottle, and became jittery as it grew empty. Our eyes held for small moments of excruciating communion—sister and brother—and then we dodged each other's gaze. What we feared more than anything was going back, going back to the darkness. Hiding in my bedroom, I thought of the crashing ocean, the beating waves. I dreamed of swimming out past the horizon to another place—the far side of the world—away from the yellow house and my father's gulping, wine-red mouth. I willed my father gone, the savagery of my thoughts my only consolation. I willed him back to the house without us. And he went, shuffling out the door.

≈

At eighteen I finished school, and moved to Brisbane to go to uni. The beach and sand were replaced with cafe lattes and concrete. Gabe, still working in his parents' business, stayed home. He visited often, and there was no talk of breaking up. I figured he would follow me when he was ready. I rented a flat on Paradise Street with my friend Lou, one of the shiny-shiny girls, and we set about making house—two country kids, wide-eyed at the newness of everything. We studied bus timetables to work out how best to get to uni, and then, flushed with triumph at our first independent bus ride, called our mothers to report back on our success. This new city world was fast-paced, and the possibilities of life stretched out before us. Study, work, travel—meeting new people, experiencing new places—and for me, freedom from the weight of all that had gone on at home. I felt I had climbed a mountain and, looking down across the vista of the city, the world was at my feet.

≈

A month after moving, I wrote my father a letter.

Dad,

It's always hard to begin a letter. It's funny because I feel like I know exactly what I want to say and then I get a pen & paper and I go blank.

There are so many things I would like to tell you about how I feel but I change my feelings so often it is difficult. I guess in a way it's because I'm so young. I'm harder and more idealistic— like that Dylan song.

I used to believe that if I could just tell you how angry you made me it would make an impact on your behaviour. That if I just told you how I felt you would change or it would help. But I don't believe that now. I know that communicating through letters can be distancing—when we could speak instead—but I think letters can also make relationships intensely intimate, and externalise things that might stay hidden. It's a form I like, and I know you do too.

Mostly, I want you to know that I never, ever in my life felt unloved by you. I don't know why Zoe felt the way she did. Perhaps her childhood was a lot different from mine? I always felt that you loved me as a child. I always felt secure. You have that to be proud of in yourself. You were such a good dad. All my early memories are happy and I always thought you were the best. This is a good achievement! Early childhood is so important, as I'm sure you know. And all is not lost! I have managed to come through this family mess relatively unscathed, and I'm sure Jake too is still a happy 'functioning' teenager.

Most fathers I know basically haven't made it through their children's adolescence with their child/parent relationships intact. I don't know whether this phenomenon is a north coast or Australian or a worldwide thing. Fathers of your generation have somehow lost out or stuffed up and I wonder if it is a side-effect of the changing gender roles, etc. I know that statement is very black and white, but it seems to me—from watching my friends—that fathers are having trouble adjusting or something.

You never told me what happened when you were hospitalised that first time. I'd like to hear it from you.

Did you ever read the story I wrote in school about how you changed? In it I described how I remembered you to be from before Zoe died—as a happy person. And you were so beautiful, Dad. It's just that one of the most beautiful things about you was the way that you listened. The way you used to listen to people—I'd watch you and think how amazing it was. I don't know if you were really listening but it always seemed so genuine. Sometimes it seems that what happened is—you stopped listening. You were so caught up in you that you stopped noticing anyone else. You didn't see us anymore, Dad.

I guess I want to say also—that I'm happy with who I am, and what I have become, and I've been able to become me through my experiences and I don't feel you have necessarily made me a worse person, or made me dislike myself. I don't feel any problems I have are due to you or your effect on me—except *as a general worry about you or about your effect on Mum.*

I know when we last spoke you said 'you're happy that I am happy'—but I know you're not. I wish you were, Dad.

I'm glad you're not working anymore. I don't think it was good for you. The trouble is—you have to find something else to do. Come back to uni and study Literature or History! I'm sure you would love it!

I still think all the time about Zoe and what she did. I can't believe that she could believe that 50 or 60 years more of life would bring no experiences worth having. Even eating a yummy meal is worth living for! And there is no way that her belief that there was nothing worth living for could have been based solely on her relationship with you. I know, deep down, that's what you think. You just must have been what was in her mind on that day when she was feeling particularly low. I hope it doesn't hurt you for me to say these things. I don't want to hurt you.

Dad, I know that Zoe devastated you. I know after that it was just hard for you to resurface. I missed you so much when you first got sick. All I wanted was for you to come back to normal. As a little child, I always believed you loved Zoe best, but it didn't bother me because I thought she was the best too. I always felt you loved me enough. I never felt neglected by you.

Dad, please don't be sad about me.

Love you, love Jessie xox

p.s. Could you tape me some really good Randy Newman and some John Lennon? I'd really love it!

Two weeks or so after I posted this letter, my father wrote back. He tore up his response before sending it, so when the envelope arrived I tipped it upside down and the fragments wafted down, fluttering over the floor of my city flat. I swept up the white paper butterflies and put them back in the envelope, then rang my mother.

'Why does he do things like that? Why send a letter ripped into tiny pieces? Does he want me to stick it back together? Is it some kind of test? I won't do it.'

'Jess, I don't know.' My mother sighed on the other end of the line. 'He's not well—he's depressed. He did a lot of things when he was … sick … He feels bad.'

'Well, I know, but why does he do things like that now? I'm throwing it out.'

'Yes, throw it out. You can't try and read a ripped-up letter.'

But I stuffed the torn letter into the back of my cupboard and tried not to think about its maimed black scrawl.

≈

When Billie finished her degree she'd moved across the sea to Japan, quick-smart. Though we'd always kept in touch, I hadn't seen much of her since Zoe's death. She remained a half-mystical creature for me. Self-sufficient, ambitious, a go-getter. Everything I was not. A few months after I left home, Billie phoned me in Brisbane, unexpectedly.

'I'll fly you over for the weekend.' Her voice was certain. 'You organise the ticket and I'll pay.'

'Are you sure?'

'Yeah, it'll be fun to have you here. Your first trip on your own. Eighteen!'

I was fresh out of home, new to the city, not yet acclimatised. Negotiating Billie in a foreign country seemed a daunting task, but I was willing. The world was beckoning—Tokyo was just the beginning. In the travel agent's, the receptionist looked at my long messy curls escaping from their tie and raised her painted eyebrows in silent question.

'My sister's flying me over for the weekend,' I confessed, feeling myself a child masquerading as an adult. An international jetsetter.

The night before I left, the phone rang. Answering it, I heard the familiar long pause and indrawn breath of my father inhaling on his cigarette.

Seconds ticked by.

'Dad. Hi.' I was impatient, halfway through packing.

'Jess.' I could hear him exhaling. I imagined the smoke drifting from his downturned mouth. It infuriated me that my father would call but not be ready to talk.

'Well, I'm almost packed to go,' I said. 'Just putting in a few more things. I'm changing money at the airport.' I couldn't bear his silence. 'Do you think that's a good idea?'

'Mmm.'

'Dad?'

'I don't know ... I'm not sure.'

I stared across at my suitcase, running through an inventory of necessities in my mind. Holding the receiver to my ear with my shoulder, I wandered across and took out a pair of socks. My father's slow smoking breath continued, floating disembodied on the other end of the line.

'Dad?'

'Yeah.'

'Are you ringing for some reason? 'Cause I'm busy now. I'm trying to get ready.'

Again, the suck on his cigarette.

'Dad?'

'Jess ...'

'Yeah?'

'Well, have a good time.'

'I hope so. I'm a bit nervous, but it'll be fine. I mean ... will it?'

The silence spread between us, jangling my nerves.

'Dad?'

'I don't know.'

'Dad, I have to go, okay? Unless you want to tell me something?'

My fingers tightened around the receiver, my knuckles turning white as I listened to his breathing.

'Dad?'

'Have a good time, Jess.'

'Yeah, okay. Bye.'

I waited for my father's slow goodbye and then hung up the phone, releasing the breath I had held while waiting for the gaps in his silence, his half-swallowed words. Turning towards my suitcase, I squashed the socks back in and then, blocking out all thought of my father, I ran back through the list in my head of everything I might possibly need.

≈

On arrival in Japan, Billie took me to lunch in the city. Tokyo: endless cement and slim, fancy-suited people who moved together like schools of fish. Anxious, I could feel my laugh becoming unnaturally loud. Telling a story, my hands swept out on either side in untidy emphasis and bumped the people cramped in beside us in the restaurant.

Billie leaned forward. 'You have to be quieter here, Jess,' she whispered. 'Just be careful—it's polite here to be considerate of the people around you.'

I pulled my arms in, chastened, wondering how I had come to take up so much space. At home I was small, but in Tokyo I was some kind of blundering giant. On the walk back from the restaurant, I saw how skilfully my oldest sister moved through the throng. Billie towered above everyone in her expensive shoes, her confidence moving her forward in life at a pace that left me straggling behind. I followed her through the crowd, still the child I had always been, trailing after my magnificent sisters, except now there was only one.

≈

The next morning Billie sat across from me at her kitchen table, buttering toast and taking neat sips from a glass of orange juice, a newspaper spread out beneath her plate. I thought about the only time I had seen her cry—after Zoe died—in the back seat of the car. There had been no sign of that kind of emotion since. I slowly chewed my toast, watching her read the paper, unsure what to say. The phone rang, cutting into the morning quiet. Billie rose to answer it, carrying her half-eaten slice of toast. She pressed the phone against her ear. *'Moshi moshi.'*

Listening, Billie whimpered like a frightened child. The triangle of toast fell slowly from her fingers. I stood up in alarm, bumping aside a chair as I moved towards her.

'What is it? What's happened?'

A low-pitched, guttural moan, 'No, no, no, no ...' Billie shook her head.

'What is it?' I hissed. 'Tell me it's not Jake.' Having lost one sibling, this was my biggest fear.

My sister's body began to convulse. She sagged towards the floor in a staggered kind of collapse. Curled up on the ground she sobbed, the phone bouncing in the air on the twisted cord.

'Billie?' I choked out.

She shook her head at me, pointing at the phone. 'Dad. It's Dad.'

I picked up the receiver. 'Mum?'

'Jess?'

'What happened?'

'He's dead.'

'He did it, didn't he?'

'Yeah.'

'How?'

'In the car, gassing himself in the car.'

'Who found him?'

'Me. I knew something was wrong when he wouldn't answer the phone, so I went round. But I knew before I got there. Jake knew too. I wouldn't let him come with me, but when I got back he was waiting at the gate, and he said just like you did, *He did it, didn't he?*' My mother's voice spilled down the phone, soft with distress.

'Is Jake all right?'

'He's here. He's okay. Quiet, you know?'

'Mum, what should I do?'

'Come home, can you come home sooner?'

I looked at my sister, shuddering on the floor. 'I'll talk to Billie. We'll work out what to do.'

'Okay, Jess.'

'Mum?'

'Yeah?'

'You'll be all right, till I get home?'

'We'll be okay, Jess.'

'Who'll pick me up?'

'I don't know, we'll think of something.'

I imagined trying to get home to my soundless, breathless father. Dead. Gassed in the car. Exhaust fumes. Carbon monoxide. My mother's silent tears.

'Okay, Mum, we'll call you back soon.'

'Jess?'

'Yeah?'

'Just … try not to be too angry.'

Numb and tingling, I was frozen in space. My sister lay unmoving below me, her fist bunched up against her swollen lips.

A rising storm was sweeping upwards through my body. I had skipped denial and gone straight to rage.

'How could he leave us when he knows what it's like to be left?' I felt myself whisper. 'He knows how this will be.'

Billie stood up, still shaky, wiping her eyes with the backs of her hands. Putting the kettle on, she slowly began to clear the kitchen bench.

Standing in the middle of her tiny apartment, I was unable to decide on the smallest movement. Motionless, not a single thought penetrated the hollow nothingness inside my mind. Billie made tea, pouring out the boiling water with an efficient flick of her wrist. I was stranded beside the phone. My sister led me over to the couch, handing me a hot cup and gesturing for me to sit down.

'You know, I'm not angry with him, Jess.' Billie was suddenly calm, sitting on her end of the couch. 'I mean, he was such a good dad.'

I tried to focus on her words.

'No matter how crazy he got, I always think of all the ways he supported us. The way he flew Zoe and me up to Burringbar every holidays when we were girls, the way he paid my rent through uni. He was always there for me, and I can't be angry with him now. I just don't feel it.'

I peered at Billie over my teacup. The anger that swelled inside me—pressing hard against my ribs—lessened just a little.

'We'll have to organise you a flight home, Jess. That's what you want, isn't it? I can't come straightaway.'

'Yes, I just want to go home.'

≈

The Tokyo subway was empty as we made our way to the platform. My wheeled suitcase clattered loudly against the cracks in the pavement as my sister and I walked together in silence. Words trailed out of arm's reach, dwindling at the edges of earshot. We were isolated in the hush of our grief, and the train station was deserted as though in response.

'I've never seen it this way.' Billie glanced about as she spoke. 'I mean, it's Golden Week, that's why.'

I couldn't answer, dragging my bag and listening to the clack-clacking of its wheels. The train to the airport was empty and I stood a moment in the open door, grasping at Billie's sad goodbye across the gap. The doors closed between us, and the train pulled away. I watched my sister recede. Identical buildings flickered past, the thwacking void of the tunnels barely registering.

On the plane, a capsule of silence moving through the night, I lay across a row of empty seats in the dark, eyes wide open but unseeing. I thought, a tearing pain within, of my father's gone-ness, of the sudden hole where he had been. My mind skipped backwards, skimming over the past years of madness and despair, landing instead in other places. The warmth and safety of my father's touch. Swimming out past the crashing waves. Clinging together while we dived under them. Knowing he would never let me go. In the blackness of that first night without him—cocooned alone in a machine in the sky—I was unable to block out the simple and undeniable question. *How could he choose to die?*

The thought somersaulted inside my mind, turning and turning, a looping refrain. And then suddenly, like the bursting of a dam wall, I remembered his voice on the phone before I left—his swallowed words, his floating breath—and I knew with the greatest certainty what it was he was calling for. He'd been trying to say goodbye.

'Are you ringing for some reason? 'Cause I'm busy now.'

'Dad, I have to go, okay? Unless you want to tell me something?'

'Yeah, okay. Bye.'

And I was flooded, silent spilling tears. I bit down on my knuckles until they stopped. Nine stretching hours suspended in the sky.

≈

It's easy to imagine that if we were to lose those we love, it would be beyond bearing. Perhaps our hearts would stop in simple protest—we could just lie down and die. But it isn't like that. Our hearts go on beating, still pumping blood through our veins. We keep taking breaths, in and out. Life as we have known it is forever ruptured, but our animal bodies are stubbornly resilient. Cells die and are replaced, vibrating matter still hums all around us, but the endless stretch of grief time begins. Minutes feel like hours, days like weeks. Around us there is action, the world flashing past, but in grief time everything is played out in slow motion.

My plane landed in Sydney, where I waited for perhaps an hour. A transit lounge. I stood and sat, and stood and sat, numbed and silent. A lone man reached for his acoustic guitar, and every song he chose slammed against me, bruising me with its surreal punch.

I thought, and not for the last time, that things are not always as you expect them to be. The strangeness of the world bustled about me, people going from one place to another, happy and unknowing. Even those who did not look happy seemed everyday and average. Yet the air had turned to oil. Movement was hindered, speech was thickened. The natural forces that held the universe together were altered, gravity had gone askew. I was spinning on a different axis, woozy and out of sync. I wanted to ask the man with the guitar to stop singing. I wanted the world around me to be still. I wanted time to stop. I wanted it to go backwards. I wanted to rewind to that place just before I'd said to my father, 'Yeah, okay. Bye.' I wanted to start again from there with a new set of questions.

'Dad, are you okay?'

'Dad, you know I love you, right?'

'Dad, is there anything I can do?'

≈

Before my father's death I hadn't been back to the house in Burringbar for over a year. Turning into that shadowy driveway on the day before his wake was like travelling along the back roads of memories so ingrained they were almost mythic. Every lazy tree folding against the car, every white pebble squashed deep within the dirt—even the grey wonga pigeons that wobbled, unhurried, along the roadside—continued untouched by the Dad-sized hole in the universe.

Walking about the garden, I slid my fingers against the prickly wooden walls of the house, caressing the palm fronds and bird's nest ferns that poked onto the walkway. The stillness was comforting, as though a peace that had been missing through the dark years had settled about the place, snuggling its arms against the buildings in a warm embrace. We had come early to clean up the house before the wake, and when we arrived we shielded our puffy eyes against the blinding light of the sun.

'It's so bright,' I muttered.

'Yeah,' my brother replied.

'It was him, then,' I whispered. 'It was him all along.'

'What?'

'He was the darkness.'

My father, who had fought the gigantean garden for years—who had battled the enormous trees and my mother's heart—trying to bring in the light, had been fighting a darkness that came from within. This darkness had gripped him, blackening the whole house, leaving it smudgy and cold and filled with shadows. We had battled it too, never really believing that he was its source, never really trusting that a man's heart could colour our whole world. Now he was dead, the brightness was so overwhelming it seemed definitive proof. Quiet fell upon us, and we wandered about, aimless and unsure. Where to begin in a dead man's home?

Our home.

My throat knotted with the emptiness of it, the word 'dead' sitting like droplets of mercury on my tongue.

At the wake I was dry-eyed but skittish with emotion. Cleaned and freshened, the house filled with people and they spilled from the sliding doors into the gardens. Almost everyone I had ever known was there. Billie, flown in from Japan just for the ceremony. Extended family I barely recognised. Gabe, Lou and the shiny-shiny girls, teachers from the school I no longer attended, all my father's colleagues and cronies and lovers and friends. The sudden presence of so many faces from the past only emphasised my father's palpable absence. And theirs. The lonely isolation that had surrounded us since Zoe's death. It was all I could do to stop myself standing on a chair and yelling, *Where have you all been?*

In his last years my father had been terrifying. Looking around at the crowds of people, it angered me that they had left us to deal with him alone. I tried not to think about all the times—after we had fled the house—that my mother had rung his friends and asked them to visit him. Frightened of him, but frightened for him too. She'd ring back the next day to see if they'd gone around, but they never had. Why was it left to us—the people he had most terrorised—to look out for him? His oldest friends had known enough to ring and tell my mother, 'Get rid of the axes. Get rid of anything weapon-like,' but they had not been willing to spend time with him, to make sure he was all right. And now here they all were at his wake, mournful and sorry.

The familiarity of every face stung, and I felt myself curl inwards, away from the sidelong glances. Wandering about, I caught glimpses of the faces of my mother, brother and sister across the way—lightning flashes of sadness—but we didn't seem to connect. Forcing myself to move through the crowd, I weaved in between the scattered groups of mourners and felt the conversation ebb to nothing as I passed.

Hours before, at my father's funeral, Zoe's long-ago boyfriend had sat in the front row and sobbed and sobbed through the service. I hadn't seen him since I was small and didn't recognise him now, grown manly and square. I couldn't understand who he was, this shattered man, his head cradled in his open palms. I was afraid, looking at him, this heartbroken stranger soaked with tears—the only person in the crowded crematorium I could not place in my father's history.

Later, at the wake, one of my father's friends introduced him:

'Romeo, here. He's turned into a man. You remember him, Jess?'

Zoe's boy smiled hesitantly.

'I didn't know who you were.' My voice came out muted.

'It's me.'

'You look different.'

'Well, you're grown up. You were a little girl the last time I was here.'

Silence stretched around us.

'I think about her all the time,' he murmured. 'She was just gone.'

'I know.'

Our words hung there in the air. My sister had been dead six years, which in grief time is nothing. A snap of the fingers, a single beat.

'It was an atomic bomb, what she did,' he said, his eyes suddenly liquid. 'Blew us all apart.'

Wine slipped from his glass onto the bricks and I felt myself nod. The ramifications of Zoe's suicide were still playing out all around us, ripples that never seemed to end. I touched my fingers to my brow—an odd compulsive gesture—and remembered Zoe's sudden sighing sprawl.

'Did you see his eyebrows, Jess?'

I wanted to flee, far away, with my hot cheeks and all my quiet despair. I pulled my hand from my face, and veered away from him in a single awkward movement, unable to say goodbye.

As the night wore on and the alcohol kicked in, people began to approach me and secrets bubbled up to the surface.

'He swallowed nails, once. He told me.'

'And shattered glass.'

So many whispered horrors.

'I know your mother was scared of him. Really scared.'

'He asked me for a threesome. Him and some woman.'

'I was so worried for Janny, for you.'

'I dreamed of him the night he died.'

'I should have visited. I knew he was in trouble.'

One of my father's cronies insisted on taking me into the garden.

'It all looks so familiar, Jess. Like I've never been away.'

The night was black, and I cringed with trepidation at the secrets he might try to tell me now that he was drunk, and he had me alone.

'Your father. Fuck. He wrote me so many crazy letters.'

My father's friends all wanted to confess what they had known, getting things off their chest. For me, this litany of secrets was too much to bear. Too many revelations all at once. Weren't they supposed to shield me from the worst of it? Hadn't I seen enough? I hung back, waiting, dreading the new information this man would want to impart. He pulled me along, and I stumbled a little on the uneven ground.

'Come on, Jess. I want to show you something.'

I followed him, unwillingly, until finally he stopped.

'Look out there. What do you see?'

I peered into the darkness. He pointed towards a densely bushed embankment in the expanse of the night and I saw what he wanted me to. There, in the distance, were two faintly luminescent spots.

'Mmm … some type of glowing mushroom?' I said. Perplexed by his urgency, I held myself stiffly against the onslaught of more furtive uttering. Another confession. I was wary, but the man was silent, staring at the two spots. He tugged again on my arm.

'No, look. It's him.'

'What?'

'It's his eyes—he's here. He's watching us.'

I looked away from the luminescent spots, gazing instead at the lights of the house, thinking of my bed in the yellow cottage by the sea. Turning, I walked back in, leaving the man swaying uncertainly in the dark.

≈

When someone you love takes their own life, they leave you with no right of reply. They have had the final say, and it is final. All the arguments you might have put forward must be swallowed. There is no one left to make them to. In suiciding, my father became both the victim and the perpetrator. The 'killed' but also the 'killer'. The kind of rage I might have felt at the murderer of my loved one—a pure, unbridled loathing—wasn't possible. I had lost him, but he had taken himself from me. And on top of that, I felt I was grieving two people—the father I had known before Zoe's suicide and the father who came after. I was a mixed-up mess of sensations—sorrow, hate, confusion, love, fear—and all these feelings had no place for resolution.

My brother and I buried my father's ashes in the garden, over-looking the orchard and the black bamboo. We tramped through the trees, our faces like masks. The ground was damp and the red soil stained the hem of my blue silk dress. Kneeling, I felt the fine fabric give way at the shoulders, the dress falling apart at the seams. Fraying and muddy, I banged the heavy dirt into the hole we had dug, covering the fine grey ash with an angry vehemence.

≈

In the days after my father's wake, my mother took long walks on the beach alone and shed weight like she was disappearing. She barely spoke. I watched her go, fretting after her fragile form. It had always been her way, to keep things to herself, but it fright-ened me to see the sudden definition of her bones beneath her skin.

'Eat something, Mum,' I cajoled, popping bread in the toaster. 'Please, just eat something.'

'I'm all right.' She crossed her arms in front of her shrinking breasts. 'I just can't yet.'

The toast I'd buttered sat untouched on the benchtop.

'I can't stomach anything,' she said. 'Not yet.'

Grief time was long. I wondered how long it would take.

Nights were the hardest. I lay awake in bed, Gabe sleeping beside me, his arm lying limp across my belly. I wanted him to wake up and help me talk, to coax the words I needed to say out of my mouth, to break into the silence that had suddenly engulfed me, but he didn't. I listened instead to the faint sound of my brother talking softly to his new girlfriend, Gemma. They'd gotten together a month or so before our father's death. Jake was sixteen and Gemma was his first love. Through the thin fibro walls my brother's words were indistinct, but I could hear his comfort, his relief, and I felt my own aloneness bang against my heart.

In the weeks after my father's death I listened as my brother and Gemma began to speak their own language, a kind of mumbled, muffled dialogue that I cocked my head to try to hear. Even though we were often in the same room, I could not comprehend their words, and my whole body strained to untangle the murmured sentences. Occasionally, I spoke up in a fit of frustration: 'What are you saying? Can I know too?' Couples are their own universe, especially in the beginning, but I felt this exclusion deeply. After my father's death, I longed for my brother's company as though he alone might understand me, but I was locked outside their tiny circle and I fought the urge to force my way in.

≈

The visceral shock of my father's suicide left me mangled. Outwardly I can only suppose I looked uninjured, but I felt as though I was actually broken—limping along, one of my arms fractured and hanging loose, my neck rigid and pained, my body grazed and raw. I felt like I had been tied to a car and dragged along behind it.

When I walked the streets of my hometown, people crossed the road to avoid a conversation. I imagined them thinking, *Fuck, I'm not up for that today.* Each one of them not knowing that almost nobody is, on any given day. That it wasn't just them avoiding me, it was almost everyone. All the times they looked away from me were adding up. There was something terribly alarming about me, something no one could face. I was becoming invisible. A shadow-walker. The wounded part of me wanted to cry out, *Why are you ashamed for me? What have I done?*

I glanced down at my body, my arms and legs, checking that I was still intact, checking that none of my brokenness was showing.

Look at me, I longed to beg. *Stretch yourself to look at me.*

But I limped on, quietly. Slipping further into the shadows.

≈

Jake and Gemma and I walked down to the shore. We stood a moment on the cool morning sand. The beach beyond the yellow cottage was long and straight, the waves rough. There was no one on the white stretch, though out in the water we could see the dotted figures of early-morning surfers. We pulled off our wrinkled sleeping shirts and tracksuit pants and—in our mismatched underwear—went down to the water's edge and let the waves rush over our toes.

'Come on. I'm going in.' Gemma's voice was gruff, sleepy.

I looked from her to Jake, searching for some inexplicable answer, but my brother's sad eyes dropped away from my gaze. Reaching out, he swept his arm around Gemma's bare waist, this small gesture his only response.

'I'm coming too.' My voice sounded hollow, as though it came not from me but from some other, faraway place.

The water was cold and I stood still, watching the goose bumps rise up my thighs and across my belly. Arms tingling, I dropped my hands beneath the cool rise of the sea. I glanced across at Jake and Gemma, and they grasped hands and dived beneath the first crashing wave, coming up together and wiping the salt from their eyes. Jake cocked his head to the side and shook the water from his ear. Gemma held the length of her hair in her fist and squeezed. I jumped beneath the next wave, resurfacing with a small splutter. I tried to steady myself, the white roar of the ocean surging towards me. Manhandled by the pummelling force of the sea, my long hair was sticky, tangling around my arms. I lost my footing and found myself pushed back in towards the shore. Crouching in the shallows, I felt the current suck at me, and I watched Jake and his girl as they swam out past the smash of the waves. In a while they washed up beside me, though none of us spoke.

'I can't escape it,' I finally blurted out. 'I feel swamped.' The sound of the waves drowned out my voice, but I tried again. 'Myself, me. I can't escape it. It's swamping me.'

Gemma looked at me, understanding flickering behind her

eyes. 'The water's rough today,' she murmured.

The current pulled at us in a sudden surge and we all scattered out along the shoreline. Staggering up, I walked back to my clothes. I shook my shirt and slid it over my head, the wind blowing prickly sand against my calves. I did not turn to watch Jake and Gemma in the shallows but kept straight on instead, heading for the yellow cottage, exiling myself from the enduring bond of my brother and his girl.

≈

Back in Brisbane for uni, I was struck down by monumental headaches that came out of nowhere, driving me to my bed. On good days, I limped through the streets of my new city world, crying behind my sunglasses. I was a stranger, and no one crossed the street to avoid me, but sorrow clung to me and I could not shake it. Gabe still visited, but I could barely raise a smile. All the methods he had refined to soothe me—feeding, snuggling, teasing—none of them seemed to work. He took to holding out his forearm and saying, 'Bite me. I know you want to. Just bite my arm.'

And I would.

'Harder. You can bite harder.'

I was afraid of hurting him, but the feel of my teeth sinking into his skin gave me a sense of release. With nowhere for my feelings to go, I had imploded. Silent on the outside, inside I was detonating. But when Gabe let me bite him, sometimes I could smile.

'You need it,' he'd say.

Taking one for the team. No one could say he didn't try.

≈

After my father's suicide, I couldn't regain my footing in the world. It was different from the way I had experienced my sister's death. Zoe had been travelling for a year and I had been used to her absence. But my father had created so much noise, so much chaos, that without him I felt suddenly plunged into empty space. Despite this, parallels between the loss of Zoe and the loss of my father were oddly present. Zoe had killed herself two weeks after I started high school, and my father took his life three months after I started university. There was a sad kind of symmetry. A feeling of déjà vu.

My flatmate, Lou, the only shiny-shiny girl who'd come with me to Brisbane, was immersed in her uni course and rarely home. In the three months I'd been enrolled at uni I'd begun a few fledgling friendships, but they were hard to sustain. How could I move through the world in such distress without explaining it? But how to explain? What words could ever convey what had happened?

Simple exchanges became fraught.

'So, what you been up to?' a new friend would ask.

Well, my father committed suicide, so there's that.

I've been having a little trouble not crying on public transport.

Actually, fuck, I think I'm going to cry now, sorry.

I didn't have the kind of relationship with anyone at university that could possibly withstand the sentences that sprang into my mind, and I didn't know what to say instead. It became easier just to avoid people altogether. In high school I'd felt alienated by this discrepancy between my inner world and my social world, but at university the incongruity was somehow worse. More jarring, less surmountable. At high school I had attempted again and again to share the realities of my experience with my peers. Mostly I felt unsuccessful. Mostly when I had spoken about my sister's death or my unravelling father, I experienced what I perceived as a withdrawal of connection or closeness. At the time I had thought it was because I didn't use the right words. I had believed that there were right words, that I just didn't know them yet. And sometimes, in some spaces, with some people, I had found comfort. Living in Brisbane, attending university, surrounded by strangers, I wasn't capable of breaching that space.

Behind in my studies, I needed to ask for extensions. I fronted up to my tutor's door and knocked.

She opened the door a fraction and poked her head out. 'Yes?'

I stuttered out my request.

'What's your excuse? This is pretty late notice.'

'Well—' I told her the bare facts through the slit in the door.

'Okay, then,' she said. 'Have another fortnight.'

The door closed in my face.

My words were unhearable. I could speak them even in the simplest, non-emotional terms, but people couldn't experience them. My father was dead and there were no words to speak right.

Refuge

I was nineteen and Gabe was twenty when we stopped using contraception. Cut adrift by grief, I looked to motherhood to soothe the pain of loss. My family had detonated—perhaps I could create a new one? I would find myself standing in the baby aisle at the supermarket, transfixed. Dummies, bottles, sippy-cups, baby blankets, those tiny, heart-rending ribbed-cotton singlets, booties, nappy-pins. I wasn't thinking of children—I was obsessed only by babies. Tiny, dependent creatures, who slept and ate and gurgled. I wanted more than anything to need those baby items, as though they were talismans from the future I might one day have. Now living with Gabe in Brisbane, I began to chart my cycle on the wall beside our bed. When did I ovulate? I needed to know. It's hard to unpick exactly what it was about babies I felt would help me. Perhaps it was as simple as a fresh start. A new human, untarnished by history. Someone I could create inside me and then sustain. Someone I could keep alive.

Once our baby was made I went to the doctor to confirm it. I rang Gabe from a phone booth outside on the street.

'It's true, I am.'

'Really?'

'Yes. Really.'

'Really?' His voice was faint and faraway on the end of the line, and I felt a flickering of unease deep within.

'Yes.'

'Right. Shit. Okay.'

I smothered the dread in Gabe's voice with all my welling hope, and from that point on we could not truly hear each other. As my belly grew and grew, we became increasingly distant— me still at uni, him off at work. At night, the words we spoke collided then slid off into the dim corners of our city home. We were slowly coming apart, a silent rending.

≈

For the first year after my father died, the house in Burringbar sat empty like the abandoned cicada shells Jake and I found snagged on trees when we were children. Dust settled in a thick layer across the surfaces and the garden encroached, branches and ferns folding in upon the house, staking a claim. In time, my mother cut away the invading trees, swept the paths clean of leaves, and moved back home to the forest from the yellow cottage by the sea. Jake had finished school and left for study and the wider world, and the house—sprawling and large—was quiet without us.

By twenty-two I'd had two babies and moved from Brisbane

back to the house of my childhood. Gabe had been unready for the challenges parenting presented. We were—the both of us— just kids, and the dream had been primarily mine. What we had seemed solid, but creating a family was a risky proposition. It was hard to predict if the structure would hold or crumble, unable to sustain the weight. Returning home with the babies was fraught, but not as fraught as leaving home had been. How rare it is for the dispossessed to regain their homeplace. When my family fled our home at the height of my father's madness, we never expected it to be restored to us. We had believed that, once gone, it was lost. Utterly and forever. Returning, babies in tow, there was a sense of welcome in the rolling hills, the endless green expanse of the forest, and the curving, bright-pebbled creek of my home.

≈

When you've lost trust, it is hard to thrust yourself again and again out into an unsafe world. All around you are unknown dangers. You don't know the topography, where to step to avoid uneven ground. In these circumstances, hiding could be seen as an adaptive behaviour. It is, after all, used to great effect throughout the natural world. Camouflage, stillness, silence, the digging of holes or hollows, or just slipping quietly out of sight. Put simply, it's one way of staying alive. In a culture obsessed by 'moving forward' or 'moving on', there isn't much space for the hibernation of grief. Even taking time to lick your wounds is often seen as an indulgence. When I retreated into motherhood and my forest home, I hid myself away from the misunderstanding of others. It was too painful to have no place in the world where my experience—the visceral reality of loss—could be honestly aired. But the forest—my homeplace—could hold my story. The forest didn't mind how mangled or broken I was. And I needed time—quiet, rhythmic, soothing—a lot of time.

I was lucky—early motherhood did provide relief from the crushing weight of my grief. It could have gone the other way. I could have ended up with two babies and felt no differently than I had before, or perhaps—terrifyingly—worse. I knew I had taken a risk, that the cost of things going wrong wouldn't be just for me, but for my children too. But as it was, the babies were so consuming I had little space for the rumination of self. Mothering offered me an emotional rest-stop, a reprieve from replaying the traumas of the past. The constancy of their needs, the relentlessness of their requirements, kept me firmly in the present moment. My very own version of a pilgrimage, of hiking some wild mountain trail. One foot in front of the other, carrying those babies, not looking away from the job at hand. But the thing about babies is they grow and grow and grow. In no time at all, they're crawling then walking, laughing then talking. They are children, asking questions you haven't figured out the answers to.

≈

Our days in the forest had taken on a gentle rhythm. Eating, walking, reading, eating, swimming, drawing, eating, reading … and swimming again. The waterhole was curved and clear, every pebble visible on the bottom. I floated on the surface of the water—arms spread wide, legs soft and drooping into the depths—watching the flitting sunshine between the leaves of trees high above. A leaf wafted down, landing softly on the water, sending ripples sweeping slowly outwards. Even in the midst of summer, the water in the shaded swimming hole was still cool enough that I had to edge in, braving the last part and plunging my head under with a gasping splash. I drifted, flat and quiet, and my children's voices echoed from the boulders, reminding me of the world beyond the lapping water at my ears.

'Mummy?' Luca called from the bank. 'My laugh has gone funny. I can't find my laugh.'

Standing up, I slid my toes against the rocky bottom. Luca watched me with large, questioning eyes, giggling goofily in demonstration.

'I love your boozies today!' he said, ever the enthusiast. My youngest son had emerged as a glass-half-full person. 'They're lovely! They look happy.'

I cupped my breasts in my hands, unable to stifle a smile. Clambering out, I sat on the bank, gathering my small son into my lap. I held Luca tightly while Milla crashed about in the water.

'Mummy?' Luca's voice was high-pitched, singsong.

'Mmm?'

'Nonny is your mummy, right?'

'Yep. Nonny is my mum.'

'Will she always live with us?' Luca tipped his head backwards to glance at my face.

My mother worked from home, sewing cushions that she sold at the local markets. It was a small but time-heavy business, and though she was always present—willing to step in if there was some catastrophe—she rarely accompanied us in our daily activities.

'I'm not sure. Maybe.'

'Our daddy lives up the coast.' Luca liked to do this, list the facts. 'But where's your daddy?'

The past, coming up to bite. The suddenness of the question surprised me, and I was momentarily without words.

'He's dead,' I said finally. It was the simplest answer I had.

Luca looked confused. 'But why?'

'He wasn't well.'

'Why's he dead?'

I had answered this question truthfully for Milla, but he was five. At three, Luca seemed still just a baby.

'He just wasn't well, but he was old, older.' The shadow of my morning headache hovered above my eyes. I didn't want to get muddled in details.

'He was old, not new?'

Luca sat a while, thinking, on my lap.

'How old are you, Mummy?'

'Twenty-five.'

'Five? Like Milla?'

'No. Twenty years older than Milla.'

'Not old?'

'No, not old.'

'You're not old, you're brand-new!'

I laughed, kissing the top of his head, swelling with gladness at his strong, supple body beneath my palms. My children's lives were so whole, so completely round, as though a circle surrounded each one, unbroken and unmaimed. Beaming faces, open and eager, blunt fringes and big eyes. Deep down, I believed they existed in a ring of safety, that they were somehow blessed, untouchable. This was irrational, I knew that, but I had to believe it to risk loving them so fiercely. Luca's question—'But where's your daddy?'—broke into our quiet world, resounding in my mind. The sadness of it overwhelmed my smile.

≈

It had been six years since my father's death, but I couldn't quite shake the sorrow of it. The immensity of his devastation—the way my father's response to Zoe's death had continuously expanded, taking up all the space in our lives—still haunted me. I was frightened of my own propensities in that regard. Could I, if I allowed myself, go down that path? My father's trajectory towards death had been terrifying. He was like a shooting star, burning wildly, crazy and then not, crazy and then not. Every decision I made after my father's suicide was based on how I could avoid his fate. The parts of him that I knew I shared—his intensity, his passion, his impulsivity, his fearlessness, his creativity, his drive—I squashed them all deep down inside.

For me, grieving had entailed a kind of disappearance. A withdrawal from the world at large, but also a toning down of self. For someone who'd once been so talkative, so expressive, I'd become more and more subdued. Watching my boys' childhoods unfold in the place where I had been a child, I was constantly reminded of who I used to be. The manhandler of biting insects who had taken on a goanna beneath a bench. So sure of the world around me, so sure of my place within it. As a child I'd been vivacious, wilful. I knew this lively part of me had become muted. I didn't believe expressing grief was a self-indulgence, but I worried that if I gave it too much room, I could lose control like my father had. In the aftermath of his suicide, I kept myself on a short leash, and perhaps with the kids there just wasn't the space.

My mother had always been quiet—private and seemingly serene. When I was a child she'd had a series of best friends, brash and opinionated, who'd never stopped talking. She'd enjoyed their raucousness, their colour and drama. But these kinds of relationships only function in fair weather, and over the years these women had all gone their separate ways. When I returned to Burringbar with my children, my mother's relief seemed almost tangible. I'm sure she would have listened to me if I'd been willing to talk about my grief, but I was loath to overwhelm her with the inner workings of my mind. It was as though

166

we had agreed at some earlier stage to shelter each other from our darker emotions. We'd both simultaneously decided: *She's been through enough, let her be.*

Whatever feelings I had I kept to myself, and over time I became more and more secretive, hiding from my mother all my saddest musings.

≈

In my bedroom, I scrambled through old letters, birthday cards, drawings and notes, searching for the familiar folded envelope of the letter from my father. I had held this envelope in my hands many times, folding it up into a square and then smoothing it out again. Inside it, creased with the lines of my sad thoughts, were the scraps of the torn-up letter my father had sent before he died, which I had never read. Finding it tucked against the bottom corner of an old shoebox, I pulled it out and folded it again into a tight square, the reflexive habit returning on cue.

In a shiny metal box, I was going to bury it.

Evading my mother, carrying the metal box and a small shovel, I took my sons out along the ridge, to my secret place. Milla raced ahead, fearless and filled with ease, but Luca clung to my legs, trembling slightly as he peered over the steep edges. I had to half-carry him down the muddy slope, the shovel clanking heavily against my ankles. At the bottom I held up the barbed wire and we slid carefully beneath. Once we'd made our way down, the boys were nimble, as I used to be, and they skipped across the rocks over the creek and onto the pebbled flat.

On the higher land above the creek, under a canopy of camphors, I began to dig.

'What are you doing, Mum?' Milla was watchful as he slid around the trunk of a tree.

'I'm burying this box. I don't want it with me anymore, but I'm not ready to throw it out.'

'But what's in it?'

Pushing the shovel into the dirt, I paused to look at my son's face. 'I can't tell you about it, Milla. It's just something that I don't want, but I can't get rid of.'

Luca wandered closer, kicking at the red dirt with his bare toes. 'Mummy, I can help. I can do some shovelling.'

'No, baby—not without shoes. You can help me put the dirt back on top afterwards, okay?'

Placing the box in the hole, I began to cover it with the damp, pebbly soil. Luca threw small handfuls while I squashed the dirt flat with my feet.

'There, now help me find a stick to mark the place.'

'A big one, Mummy?'

'One I can wedge into the ground, so I don't lose the spot.'

Milla strolled over from his tree with a long, slightly curved stick.

'But I thought you didn't want what's in the box,' he said. 'Why do you need to know the spot?'

'I just do, that's all.'

I stood a moment beside the stick, wondering if the damp

soil would turn my box to rust and knowing that a flood would wash it all away. I imagined the metal box wedged between the branches of a tree on some lone farmer's land.

'Come on, boys—let's go for a wander.'

Leaving the shovel propped against Milla's tree, we headed downstream, watching for stray pieces of barbed wire and the low, thorny bushes that always caught against our clothes.

All along the creek edge grew straight-leaved plants that thrust from the ground like pompoms. Covered in moss, boulders were strewn about, ferns growing from their dirt-crammed pockets. When I was a child I'd seen these rotund bodies as alive, as entities with their very own dispositions: serious or jolly, comforting or cold. From where I stood with the boys, the roots of the forest trees lay exposed in cross-section, part of the ever-changing creek bank. I could see their private underworld in all its intertwined layers—years and years of connectedness and union—changing but unchanged. My secret place, out beyond the ridge.

We walked along the banks of the creek, weaving on and off the well-trodden cow paths. Luca stopped to poke at the water with a stick, stirring up mud, and Milla looked across at me as though searching for something.

'Mum, what was in the box?' His face was tilted. Watching me, he pulled at his bottom lip with his top teeth.

My children always seemed to be studying me for clues to some great mystery I could never explain.

'It was something private, something sad.' I heard myself

sigh. 'Something I'm not ready to share.'

'A secret?'

'Yeah, baby. A kind of secret.'

Milla shuffled towards me, wrapping his arms around me and leaning against my hips, restrained and tender. Catching sight of us, Luca dropped his stick into the creek and ran across to squeeze in against his brother, working his way into the embrace like a wriggling puppy. Both boys pressed against me until they began to jostle, and I nudged them from my arms and turned to head back.

≈

My brother visited sometimes with Gemma, a weekend away from uni. He came to see us, but he never said much. I was struck by how quickly Jake curled into the couch of our childhood, as though once home he slotted straight back into the habits of his adolescence. Despite the boisterous excitement of my children, quiet swirled around him, like the notes from his guitar. I had to hold my tongue for long stretches to hear him speak.

'I liked that CD you gave Mum,' I told him. 'The Lucinda Williams.'

'Yeah ... it's ... good.'

'It's really atmospheric, but so sad.'

'It's ... it's got that ...' My brother's voice fell away. 'When you listen to it ...'

I had to stop myself from filling all Jake's pauses with my

own thoughts, from talking and talking so that the silence did not hang between us.

'It kind of …'

'Yeah?'

'It just …'

'Makes you feel …?' I asked, inclining my head in encouragement.

'Makes me … want … yeah …'

I tried to leave room for my brother's words, but he did not step forward to fill the gap. I wanted to give Jake space to be, but it always seemed that the space I allowed just became more space between us. A void where my words used to lie. I wanted to step up and fill in all the gaps, to join together all the missing parts and tape up all the broken edges. I wanted to bridge the place where the unspoken lay: the abyss, the hidden chasm between him and me.

Brother and sister.

In his company, the clamour of the unspoken filled my ears— the clanking, banging, shifting machinery of all those words left unsaid. Two minds at work avoiding the unploughed ground. Weed-infested spaces had grown between us where all our secret sorrows were buried. Underground, deep underground. I wanted to burrow beneath the surface to these hidden chasms, but instead was solitary and still, waiting for the outstretched arms of my brother. I waited for Jake to reach out and give me balance, to hold me steady while I stepped forth and crossed that bridge between us. I saw the unspoken hovering behind my brother's eyes, and I waited and waited for those small, unbroken moments when the chasm between us would be breached.

≈

Since coming home I had avoided people I saw on the street the way they had once avoided me, averting my gaze, going about my business. I believed myself to be lost to them, someone who'd become separated from the flock. I knew it had all started with awkwardness and not from a lack of love, but how long after someone's father suicides is conversation with them discomfiting? In my experience—quite a long time. I appreciated those who had taken that plunge into awkwardness, though they were few and far between, and every friend who had called me after my father's death would stay forever etched into my memory, just for being willing to listen to my sad voice on the other end of the line. Bravery comes in so many forms, but this has to be one of the most overlooked. We celebrate those who have climbed high mountains or broken into burning buildings, but try calling your friend who has just lost her baby and listen to her keen. I know how hard these moments can be. I have experienced them now from the other side, more times than I would have ever expected.

Why do we find the pain of others so difficult to bear? Nowadays, I think of our country's asylum seekers, locked away in detention centres, sewing up their mouths or lighting themselves on fire. They're trying to make their suffering visible, but the more they do it, the more likely we are to look away. I wonder about this collective mercilessness. I know that it is in some part a feeling of helplessness, but the outcast within me wonders how much of it is also a fear of contagion. We make them live on the other side of the river, like the lepers of old, so we don't have to witness their pain. If we really looked at these people, what would we see? Does their brokenness somehow reflect our own? Or, at the very least, our own potential for it? Or is it the other way around? In acknowledging their suffering, will we find we've been complicit in it? Will it require something of us that we feel unable to give?

≈

There are different routes to choose when it comes to the expression—the outward expression—of who you are, and what your story might be. Conversations can lead quickly to topics like siblings and parents, so if you want to communicate about those things the opening is often there. But if you don't want to communicate about them—or don't know how to—then you must, from the outset, avoid whole major areas of conversation. Looking back, I think this was often the path my siblings took.

Many years after my father's death, I went to Japan to visit Billie, and while I was there she invited a close Australian friend over to her house for lunch. My sister was fussing in the kitchen, and her friend said to me, 'So, when did you appear?'

We were sitting at the dining room table. It was a small open-plan Japanese house and I assumed my sister could hear our conversation from the kitchen, but she didn't show any sign of registering the question.

'What do you mean?' I asked, a touch confused.

'When did you appear in Billie's life? When did she discover you?'

It dawned on me then that this friend thought I was some long-lost sister who'd turned up late, who'd just appeared out of nowhere.

'Oh, no, I've been here from the beginning,' I said quietly. 'I've been here all along.'

I looked across at Billie, understanding in that moment that she hadn't told her friend anything about me. Though she had lived so far from me, and for such a long time, Billie had always worked hard to stay in touch, to maintain our connection, despite her intensely busy life. She had never made me feel that I was not an important part of her family, and yet she had managed not to mention my existence to one of her best friends in Japan. I knew why—because as soon as she talked about me, she'd end up having to talk about Zoe, and then probably Dad. And if she didn't want to talk about Zoe or Dad, or she felt that there wasn't room for that conversation in her friendship, then she had to avoid talking about me too, if she didn't want to outright lie.

'Oh, right,' my sister's friend said, glancing towards Billie. 'Well, so, how many of you are there?'

I knew this was an important moment, and I knew my sister had thus far avoided it. I wasn't sure what I should say. I was happy to answer the question however Billie wanted me to, but she didn't give me any sign from the kitchen.

'Well, there were four of us, altogether,' I said, tentatively.

My sister's friend raised her eyebrows in surprise. 'Oh, right,' she said again. She paused. 'So what are the others doing now?'

I went through it with her: Zoe and me and Jake. I could see both her shock and her understanding. It was all there in her face, the fact that she knew why Billie had never mentioned me, and the fact that she knew—right then and there—the kind of painful hidden past that my sister must carry but never ever spoke of.

So that's one way to manage that conversation—just never to have it. To let people assume that you don't have a family. I've had similar experiences with my brother, going to visit him when he lived in share houses. I'd turn up, and his flatmates would think I was his new girlfriend, and they might be different shades of enraged because he already had a girlfriend, and I'd have to explain that I was a sister who he'd never mentioned.

I have never been surer of anything than that my siblings love me, that they value me and are glad I'm in the world, but the story of my family is so hard to tell that sometimes it's been easier for them not to tell it at all, even when they know I'm going to visit them and no one is going to understand where I came from. This is the conundrum of the grief-laden, the conundrum of those with stories too hard to tell and too difficult to bear hearing. It is easier to reinvent ourselves unhindered by our history in a new city. Our whole past just disappears, evaporating behind us as we walk. It's a road that both my siblings took, or have taken from time to time, but it's not a road that I could take. In erasing my past, I would be erasing my dead ones—Zoe and my father—who in life had loomed so large. I didn't want to live as though they had never existed.

In my homeplace, I wanted to live with my story. I didn't want start again somewhere fresh and pretend it never happened. I wanted it to be visible behind me, not evaporating into the air so everyone else got to feel more comfortable. But I didn't know how to breach that space. I lived, nestled in the forest—held, loved, connected—but walking the streets of my hometown I felt potently the opposite. Belonging, it seemed, was conditional. In grief I felt myself to be cordoned off, I had become an untouchable.

Many years later I read about studies that found the lonelier a person is the more likely they are to interpret social cues negatively. To see themselves as rebuffed or unwelcome. But because this shift into loneliness is often incremental, these changes in perception are not at all apparent to the person suffering them. The lonely person is caught in a cycle, seeing rejection everywhere and withdrawing rather than reaching out, compounding their isolation. It struck me that this must happen very quickly in cases where a person has experienced something that is difficult to approach in conversation—rape, sexual abuse, mental illness, the murder or suicide of a loved one, or just plain and simple loss. Awkwardness is a small thing in comparison to the kinds of troubles that incite it, but humans—for the most part—seem intent on avoiding it at all costs. How many avoided interactions does it take for the lonely person to start seeing them everywhere? To start avoiding being avoided?

≈

In our daily meandering, I spent a lot of time wondering what to say to my children about my family history. I worried that suicide ran in families, that once one person fell, others would topple, as if suicide had become an option. I didn't want my sons to see taking their own lives as a viable solution, but I also didn't want my history to be a secret they uncovered later. I didn't want them to feel they'd been lied to, that their childhoods were built on something false. I knew the questions would come, and I tried to be ready.

On a drive to the shops, I glanced at my boys in the rear-vision mirror.

'Mum, why does Billie live in Japan?' Milla asked out of the blue, searching for my eyes in the mirror.

'She has a fancy job there. In a big company.'

'Will she ever come back here to live?'

'I don't think so. She likes living in the city.'

'What about your other sister, the one who's dead?' In the back of the car Milla was suddenly alert. 'What's she called again?'

Luca listened, but didn't speak.

'Zoe was her name … Billie and Zoe.'

Holding my breath, I waited for the next question.

'But how did she die, Mum?' Milla asked.

It seemed to me that the truth was my only option. The raw truth: *It happened, it was like a bomb dropping, no one was unscathed.*

I breathed in and out, slowly, wanting to reply but not knowing how.

'She killed herself—'

I scanned Milla's face in the mirror. He looked thoughtful, pensive.

'Like your dad?'

I'd already had a conversation with Milla about my father's suicide. He knew the basic facts.

'Yes, like my dad.'

Milla peered out the window. I could see Luca's gaze slip back and forth between us. I'd avoided telling Luca that part of the story at the creek. There in the car, I didn't know what else to say, what to explain and what to leave out. My boys were five and three, too little for the details. I wound down the window to feel the wind in my face.

'But Mum ...' Luca finally spoke up, his voice uncertain, tremulous. 'Why?'

The unanswerable question hung in the air. Heavy with sorrow it hovered about us, filling our ears and our minds and our hearts.

≈

I had always experienced occasional headaches, but after my father's death they had become almost ever-present. I often woke with a dull pain behind my eyes that persisted steadily until I readied myself for sleep. I went to different specialists over time, and the diagnosis was always 'tension headaches'. When I asked if this was stress-related—that is, if 'tension' equalled 'stress'—no one seemed to think so. Simple painkillers, paracetamol and the like, were prescribed. It didn't feel right to take painkillers all day every day, so I limited myself to two paracetamol tablets once a day. Mostly I chose to take them right before bed, so I could drift into a pain-free sleep.

The headaches bothered me, but they also seemed somehow normal. An outward expression of how I felt inside. Sometimes the pain drifted into a migraine, blurring my vision, wiping me out. But that was less common. Living with chronic pain is a half-life—everything is muted, shrouded in a kind of fog. I tried all kinds of home remedies: heat-packs, homeopathics, herbal teas and supplements. Nothing worked. In the scheme of things—the relentlessness of mothering small children—my headaches were background until they were foreground. A presence, always lingering, but sometimes rising up to knock me out.

The afternoon George arrived I was suffering. I'd had a migraine the day before and was finding it hard to resurface. George was an old city friend of my father. When I was a child he would appear on our doorstep from time to time, bringing with him a small band of drinkers. They were a raucous bunch, full of outlandish stories. They'd sit around the kitchen table

179

and talk politics and women and sex, and my mother was always shutting the door so we didn't have to hear. As a child, I'd liked them all, these madcap men, though George was my favourite. He was a writer who'd spent a lifetime writing non-fiction books on obscure topics that were never published. He drank beer for breakfast and laughed so much his face was set in permanent smile lines. He was Czech, and apparently his own father laughed so vigorously he often fell flat on his back.

Occasionally, when I was a kid, we'd visit George in Brisbane. He lived in a sectioned-off part of his long-suffering mother's house. In his bathroom, he had a photograph of his own penis on one side of the basin and on the other the vagina of a girl-friend. As kids, these genital portraits were right at our eye level, and we'd inspect them with curious mirth. In the rest of the house he had perfect skeletons of frogs and lizards mounted behind glass and arranged on the walls, and there was an indoor climbing vine that had almost taken over the rafters. In another life he'd practised as a psychologist, and my father once told me the coffee table in his waiting room had a glass top with a giant horse's penis below it that was slowly decaying.

After my father's death, George rarely visited. The gang of drinkers had mostly disbanded, and I assumed he didn't like to be reminded of my father's messy demise. On the day after my migraine, he turned up unexpectedly. He was subdued, not laughing, muttering every now and again, 'Oh, it's a terrible thing, your father. A terrible thing.'

This was a fact, though it had been six years since my father's death. In the aftermath of my migraine, my children's voices seemed loud and demanding, and George's grief was a little hard to bear.

It bothered George that I hadn't finished university. That I had chosen the forest and babies over books and the world.

'It's such a shame. She can't just do this with her life,' he'd say to my mother, indicating our house with a sweep of his arm, taking a long sip of his beer. 'It's a waste—she's got brains.'

I explained to him about my headaches. Evidently, I'd never mentioned them before.

'But that's untenable,' George said, shocked. 'I mean, it's no good.'

George liked to solve problems. The psychologist in him. He asked me a bunch of questions about my pain, and then declared he might have the answer.

'Alexander Technique is what you need,' he stated firmly. 'I have a book about it. I'll send it to you.'

A week or so later I got the book in the post, searched the Yellow Pages for a practitioner and made an appointment. It seemed a whim. Nothing had worked in the past. I had no real expectation of the alleviation of my pain, but I dutifully made the appointment. I don't know why I needed crazy George of all people to tell me my pain was untenable, but it seemed that I did.

≈

The Alexander practitioner had a private studio out in the hills, which was unusual but not unheard of. Varda was diminutive in stature but large in presence, with expressive, vibrant blue eyes. She welcomed me, and we had a chat about my headaches. As the conversation wound down, she said, 'Often pain in the body is related to our emotional experiences. I'm also a trained counsellor. Is there anything about your life you'd like to share?'

I stared at her a moment, trying to read the situation.

'Well,' I murmured. This openness was unprecedented. 'There are a few things ...'

I offered up the bare bones of my story. Varda's eyes widened and I looked away. I had overshared, again, and now she would wish she hadn't asked. I glanced back, deeply apprehensive, but she held my gaze.

'I have a lot of experience with trauma,' she said steadily. 'This is a safe space, and I'd like to hear your story.'

I didn't think of myself as someone who had experienced trauma. I associated it with wars, soldier PTSD. Some things had happened, yes. But shouldn't I be over that by now?

'No one likes to hear about it,' I said warily. 'It's way too intense.'

'That's not a problem for me. I like intense.'

This in itself was a revelation.

'You do?'

Varda nodded, her gaze direct. I could see that she was thinking.

'It's as though your adolescence is in brackets,' she said,

holding up two hands to illustrate. 'Your sister's death at the beginning and your father's at the end.'

I nodded, still in shock that someone was willing to discuss it.

After this initial appointment, I went back fortnightly. And so it began, a detailed recounting. Varda gave me permission to speak of what I had thought to be unhearable. She allowed space for whatever words came out, whatever memories came up, and the sense of wrongness in my communication that I had carried with me so long began to dissipate in her presence. She said: 'Sorrow is a terrain you can enter and leave. You can explore it, but you aren't stranded there.' She said: 'I will go with you.' She said: 'You can call me any time you get stuck.' And she was always true to her word.

≈

When I first met Varda, I had lost faith that there was a language I could speak that could be heard. Outside of the forest, I felt like a person stranded in a foreign land where none of the words I used made any sense. Whenever I tried to broach a topic that was meaningful to me, I felt I was speaking gibberish. In grief, language itself seems to fragment. If, on top of that, no one can hear you, the sense of dislocation is compounded. I had become resigned to this feeling of misunderstanding or remoteness, the blankness of people's faces in response to my words, but it hurt me greatly to move through my life so unheard. It is hard to overstate the importance of being able—after so many years of silence—to simply speak. I didn't know how much I needed someone to bear witness to the happenings of my life, but when I met Varda and she looked into my eyes, the shadow-walker in me—that terrifyingly wounded being that had no place in the world—came forward. At first that part of me was timid, expecting to be repulsed, but Varda was undaunted. I talked about everything—my sisters, my father, my mother, my brother, my children, Gabe, the lot. There wasn't anything that Varda could not hear.

Every fortnight she would coax me onto her table and try to help my body release some of the strange tension it held. There was no massage, but a light lifting of limbs with some verbal instructions. 'The neck releases the head, forward and up ...'

It was normal, apparently, for emotion to be released along with this tension, and Varda would often ask me what I was feeling. So unused to the question, mostly I wouldn't know. She would ask me then about any images that came to mind, any memories or thoughts. And this would lead—always—right back to my childhood. Varda chose her words carefully, each one imbued with a very specific meaning. I'd never met someone so particular about language. Intelligence hummed in the air around her, almost electric. I found myself listening closely to each word she spoke.

When Varda said, 'Try writing some things down,' I listened. I started writing in secret at first, as I did most things, but the words came tumbling out. In writing, there was no uncomfortable silence, no awkwardness, no withdrawal of connection, just the open space between what was in my head and what was on the page, and the liberation of it was giddying.

≈

I stood in the shower, water streaming down my body, a delicate blanket of lines. Sliding my feet across the tiles, I looked up to feel the heat against my forehead. The seconds spun by— spiralling time—my life measured in small heartbeats. The flicking of my fingernail against the wet skin of my thumb, the sunlight glowing through the underside of leaves, the repeating bird sounds that blended in the back of my mind. I thought about the terrain of sorrow, how I could come and go. I had spent so long at home in the forest, but since meeting Varda I'd started wondering about the world outside. She was a practitioner, yes. A therapist. Talking to me was her job. But maybe there were other people out there who liked intensity as much as she did? Maybe there was a tribe?

Looking out at the garden sea, I leaned over and traced the letters of my name in the misty steam of the glass. I existed. Varda had heard me speak, and maybe there were others.

≈

The thing about hiding is that eventually you have to emerge. You can choose safety over risk as long as you wish to, but it will limit your experiences. Connection with others is a balm, and for me this connection had become sorely lacking. In town on a summer break, the shiny-shiny girls—my brainy high school pals—swooped in from their busy city lives to visit, whisking me out to a local pub in a seaside tourist town not far from the green garden sea, but the riotous clatter of the place was overwhelming. In school we'd all been going in vaguely the same direction, but since then our paths had diverged. At the pub these old friends were as lively as ever, but I found a corner and stuck to it stubbornly until they agreed to take me home.

Out in the world, I often felt panicked. There were none of the things that in the forest were grounding or safe-feeling. Most specifically trees, but also animals and the movement of nature: the wind shifting around me, the flickering of insects and the flashing of birds—the gentle sway of things. I found these natural rhythms immensely comforting. But it was also the way these entities reached out and touched me. To go anywhere—to the toilet or my bedroom—I had to move through the wilderness. As I walked, the plants brushed my arms. I got leaves and things stuck on me. In just wandering about, I was entering into a connectivity with nature that felt lively. It's easy enough to say you 'brush past' a tree, but somehow it felt more like the trees were reaching out and touching me, caressing me with fondness. With the absence of these entities, the world outside my home had come to feel deeply foreign.

Varda suggested that I'd 'trauma-bonded' with my home-place, the way an abused woman does with her partner. Trauma bonding, she explained, occurred as the result of ongoing cycles of abuse: intermittent reinforcement of reward and punishment creates powerful bonds that are resistant to change. But Varda had never been to my house. She hadn't known the tender embrace of my forest. Cycles of abuse? There were seasons—cyclical, yes— and sometimes storms and floods. Occasionally, it even hailed. But this place had loved me doggedly since I was the smallest child. It was where I experienced the loss of Zoe and where my father went mad and where everything I knew of family had collapsed in on itself and exploded—and yet at the same time it was where I felt most held and most understood and most myself. We'd grown here together—the forest and I—planted by my parents, and we were intertwined: a support system of inter-linking branches, holding each other upright.

Despite this, there was always room for the unexpected. One day, when I was going down the walkway to my bedroom, a large swarm of bats began flying up and down the passage. They were small but vigorous, fluttering right up into my face and chest. I stood still, head ducked, hand shielding my eyes, waiting for them to settle or disperse. Caught in an unforeseen moment, unprepared and vulnerable. Suddenly I was living inside a bat colony. I had to walk the gauntlet of bats before I could enter or exit a room. It hadn't been the case the day before. See how everything could change in the blink of an eye? In the forest, every day things grew or died. Nothing was static. Some days, a lone butterfly would waft in from outside and land upon me for the merest second, and then be gone. Over the years, I had awoken with doves on my head, snakes curled in the bottoms

187

of my cupboard drawers, toads in the shower, and the translucent underbellies of frogs pressed up against the glass of my
doors. Once trapped inside, the frogs became dry, entangled in
spider webs and dust, and I had to scoop them up, running them
under a tap until—clean and moist—they were ready to go back
outside. The constant knock of nature on my door, an earthen
rhythm of syncopated heartbeats.

There was no other choice but surrender.

≈

After my terror at the noisy pub with the shiny-shiny girls,
I thought I'd try something easier and I drove with Milla and
Luca to the beach. The boys sat in the back, watching the flickering of the trees outside, enveloped in the early-morning hush.
For this outing, I'd chosen with care from the curving coastline
east of my home. I'd avoided the white sands and brisk winds
of my childhood and driven instead to an unfamiliar, neutral
stretch of sea. Milla and Luca raced from the car, across the
prickly grass, and along the sand to the water.

In the rush to get out of the house I had left the bag with
all the towels and hats and drinks at home by the door, and
so arrived light and unhindered by seaside paraphernalia. The
beach was quiet, and a little way off a man stood fishing.

Milla plunged into the water, laughing and splashing. Luca
inched in slowly, staying in the shallows, keeping his head up
and dry. Sitting on the sand, I watched my two boys in the water.

Milla romped in the surf, going out further and further, until I had to stand and call him in, while Luca skipped about at the shoreline, jumping the frilly waves and occasionally submerging his little body in their ebbs and flows. I couldn't relax with my two boys so far apart, and found myself panicking every time Milla went under a wave. Walking to the water's edge, my gaze followed my older boy's form. Milla was a robust swimmer, and the waves were not rough. Watching him play in the sea, something tight within me gave way, and I dug my feet into the sand.

Luca scrambled along the shore picking up shells and digging haphazardly. He approached the lone fisherman. I knew he would be asking something. *Why are there waves? How is there sand?* The man smiled down at him and then up at me in reassurance. I wondered if I should bring Milla in from the waves and rescue the fisherman from Luca's tireless inquiries, but the man laughed then, a deep, warm sound.

The waves lapped at my ankles and splattered up to wet behind my knees. I was wearing a simple green sundress and I tucked it up so the waves wouldn't splash the hem. As I watched Milla in the surf, my mind flew off towards the blue line of the horizon. I breathed out in a sigh.

Suddenly I heard Luca's high-pitched scream.

'Fuck, fuck, shit!' the man shouted. 'Mate, show me your hand.'

I ran towards them. The fisherman was holding my son's whole hand firmly between his palms. 'He grabbed the hook when I was reeling it in,' he hissed. 'Shit! Hold him still while I try and get it out.'

I pulled Luca towards me, my eyes blurring with tears. The fisherman tugged tentatively at the wedged hook. Luca screamed.

'Fuck, it's all the way through. Fuck … fuck,' the man muttered.

Luca shrieked even louder, white with fear. Milla scrambled in from the surf and stood beside me.

'Mum, what are you going to do?' The corners of his mouth turned down. 'Mum?'

I shook my head, a small sob escaping from some deep place inside me. When either of the boys got hurt, it broke the circle I believed surrounded them, the circle of safety. The very idea of their vulnerability undid me. Accidents, illnesses—I felt the world was coming apart. All that trauma coming up to bite.

I swiped at my eyes with the back of my hand. The man looked at my face, then back at Luca's finger with the barbs of the hook protruding.

'Okay, mate, just wait, one more try.' Delicately, the fisherman grasped the base of the hook. He gave it a sharp, hard wrench and the metal barb came free. My son's finger trickled blood and I scooped him up and whispered to him as I cried against his hair. The man stood there watching us, his face pale and sad and sorry. In my arms, Luca was quiet. Milla stayed close beside me, dripping and quivering.

The fisherman reached out and placed a palm on top of Milla's head. 'It's okay, mate. He's okay,' he said softly.

I shifted Luca onto my hip so I could pull Milla into my embrace. He fell into me, pressing his face into my sodden sundress. Squeezing him, I tried to stop crying. 'It's okay, baby—it's not that bad,' I whispered. 'It just gave Mummy a fright.'

'He put out his hand and grabbed the hook,' the man said. 'So quick I couldn't stop him.'

'It was an accident,' I sniffed. 'He doesn't know about fishing. He wouldn't have known there was a hook on the end.'

'Come on, mate—give us a look at your finger. See if you need a bandaid.'

Luca turned his face from my shoulder, holding his pierced finger wrapped like a treasure in his other hand.

The fisherman gently pried away Luca's small fingers. 'Not too bad, but it's bandaid material. I've got a first-aid kit in my car. You want to come up and I'll fix it for you?'

Luca's bottom lip began to tremble, his eyes brimming again with fresh tears.

'Luca?'

Tilting his head back in abandon, my son pushed his lips together like a tiny sad bird, but he nodded. Watching his delicate face, I couldn't keep from crying, and as we walked up the beach to the fisherman's car, I hid my tears in Luca's hair.

The car was a banged-up old ute, and the fisherman motioned for me to sit down in the passenger seat. Edging myself in against the torn upholstery, I held Luca on my lap as Milla huddled in worriedly against my knees. The fisherman walked to the back of his ute, returning with a towel for each of my boys and a large metal first-aid chest.

'Come here, mate, and I'll wrap you up,' the man said to

Milla, and my son stepped away from me into the towel. The fisherman handed me the other towel and I draped it over Luca's shoulders.

'Thanks,' I whispered, sniffing softly, trying to rein myself in.

Putting the metal chest on the bonnet of the ute, the fisherman opened the lid. Both the boys watched in awed silence. They had never seen a first-aid kit. The fisherman washed Luca's injured finger with disinfectant, then dabbed it lightly with white cream. Luca made his purse-lipped-sad-bird face, but he kept very still. With great solemnity the fisherman produced a narrow white bandage and then wrapped Luca's finger with slow, careful movements, winding the end of the bandage around Luca's palm and finally tying it in a neat, tight knot.

Like the boys, I had been in thrall to the seriousness of this bandage procedure, but once it was done the situation seemed slightly farcical and I found myself smiling at the man's grave face. He bent forward to check his handiwork, then glanced up and grinned at me with gleaming black eyes. My breath sucked up inside me at his smile. Startled, I wondered if my own dark eyes looked anything like his. It struck me that this man was very beautiful, with his kind face and gentle hands, and I tried to guess how old he was.

'Well, boys, that's some fancy bandaid,' I said. 'Thanks, thanks a lot. That was awful, wasn't it?' My voice was wet but unduly cheery.

'Yeah. Shit, you know?'

Holding Luca tight, I clambered out of the fisherman's ute. Caught in this sudden intimacy with a stranger, I wasn't sure what to do.

'Come on, boys—let's go, hey? Let's go home.'

'Wait a minute,' the fisherman said. 'Sit down a sec on the grass, get your bearings.'

A pulse still beat in the back of my head, tears prickled behind my eyes. Perhaps I should wait and not jump straight into the car? Torn, I looked down at the grass.

'Okay.' I stood Luca on the ground at my feet and wrapped him snugly in the towel, then sat down and pulled him onto my lap. Milla stood beside me, the towel flapping off his shoulders, his gaze on the water.

'Mum, can I go back in?'

'Hmmm, but I'm all the way up here.'

'Just in a little bit?'

'Only if you stay right at the edge. No swimming, just paddling.'

'Up to my knees?'

'Yeah.'

Milla ran down to the shore. He jumped the shallow waves, the water splashing up against his belly. I could see him restraining himself from going in any deeper, and he turned back to check I was watching. Wriggling on my lap, Luca loosened the towel. He watched Milla, as though an imagined game between them continued unabated in his mind. The fisherman sat down beside me on the grass and the three of us were silent, watching

Milla play. After a moment Luca stood and shook off his towel. He lingered a little at my crossed knees, then turned to face me with large, sombre eyes.

'Mummy, my finger doesn't hurt anymore,' he said, as though I might not believe it. 'Can I go down and play with Milla?'

'Yeah, baby—just try and keep the bandage dry.'

Luca wandered down to the water. He called out to Milla in his high singsong voice, then he too jumped over the small waves and laughed as the water sprayed up against his body.

'They play well, your boys.'

I was alert to this man beside me, with his tattered rolled-up jeans and his strong, bristled forearms, but I was still startled by his statement, the beginning of a conversation I wasn't quite expecting.

'Yes, they've always been like that. It's as though they just fit each other's little nooks and crannies. It's lucky, I suppose.'

'My kids fought like demons when they were little.'

'Yeah?'

I looked across at the man's face, slipping a family into the picture of him that was forming in my mind. He was perhaps thirty-five, I thought, with a wife and three kids. The man smiled, his lips turning up on one side, but his eyes slid away from mine. He was subdued now, after all the drama of the embedded hook, and I was enlivened.

'Thanks for looking after Luca like that,' I said. 'They were very impressed by your first-aid kit. Does every fisherman carry one of those in the back of his ute?'

'I don't know, really. I'm sorry about the hook.'

His words seemed to edge quietly towards me in the wind.

'I'm always like that,' I said. 'When it's them, my boys, I just can't hold it together. You're supposed to have a rush of adrenaline or something that makes you … capable of reacting, but I just … fall apart at the seams. It's bad—' I paused. 'I mean, it must upset them, it must make them more frightened.'

'It was nasty, that hook in his finger.' His voice was soft. 'It was all the way through.' He looked off towards the boys still bounding about the shore. 'It made me feel sick, and he's not even my kid.'

I pulled out a blade of grass and broke it into pieces, arranging them in a green flower on my bare knee, knowing I should say something more. I'd been out of the world for some time, and these first steps back were wobbly, unpractised. If I'd ever had any grace in company, I had lost it. I felt like a broken bird after a long convalescence, trying clumsily to relearn how to fly.

The fisherman shifted there beside me, as though he too felt a restless unease.

'Sometimes I feel like the only person left on earth, besides the boys,' I blurted out. 'When I think of myself from the outside, I know I must cut the loneliest figure.' The words kept tumbling from my mouth. 'It feels like the edge of the world just here, don't you think?'

I blushed, looking away. I hoped he wasn't watching me. I felt the sudden heavy presence of my own body. Conscious of myself sitting there beside him, I stood up, crossing my arms over my breasts, wondering if I could just walk away.

'What about your bloke? Where's he?'

I stared at my bare feet in the green grass, not knowing how to explain.

He crossed the ocean a while back.

'He's gone now.' I felt myself sigh, teetering there on the brink of appropriate conversation. 'I was with him so long, and when I had the babies he just sort of slipped away. I mean … slowly, and after a while it was like there wasn't anyone left.' I had plunged right over, but continued on, doggedly. 'He seemed almost empty, and I used to prod him, you know, to see if I could find him again. After a while I made him leave—it was lonelier with him there.'

I'd been silent so long, but suddenly I was spilling words. Dread was rising inside me. I feared I would be struck down for the folly of sharing such secrets. I waited for this man to get up and leave. To say, *Well, this started out okay, but enough is enough.*

He was quiet. Thinking. Finally he said, 'Sometimes I think I'm like that. Like there's nothing left inside me.'

I glanced up at his eyes. They were sad and unflinching. He didn't break my gaze. I began to tremble and couldn't stop. I hugged my arms about myself, fighting the urge to flee.

'Do you come here much?' I asked, not wanting to be rude, wishing to be friends.

'Yeah, I live not far off. I haven't seen you here before.'

'I've never been to this beach. It's nice. Peaceful.'

'Yeah.'

I felt myself step back, edging away from the man before me, starting to panic. 'Look, I'm just going to check on my boys.'

Turning and walking down the grassy slope to the sand, I stiffened against the man's gaze on my back. I couldn't help bracing against the idea of his eyes upon me and felt juvenile and ashamed. When I reached the boys they were fine. Luca's bandage hung limp and forlorn from his hand.

'I accidentally got it wet, Mummy.'

'It doesn't matter—we'll fix it up when we get home.'

I looked up towards the man, and he waved. Standing, he walked down to the sand and back to his discarded fishing gear. I watched him a moment, then forced myself to walk across to him—to be polite, to say goodbye.

'I'm going to go in a minute.' I tried to be normal, whatever that was. 'Thanks for everything. Thanks for the towels. I'll put them in the back of your ute when I go.'

Nodding, the man was somehow defensive. This stranger, with the kind face and the first-aid kit. I knew that by sharing I had invited him to speak, then promptly run from his honesty. I stood, awkward and sorry, swiping the sand with my toes.

'Maybe I'll see you again one day,' I said. 'It was good to talk to you.'

'Yeah. What's your name?'

'Jessie.'

The fisherman grinned then and pointed to the sand at my feet. I'd drawn a large circle about myself.

'Are you defining your boundaries?'

I laughed, an unexpected springing giggle.

'Well, don't worry, Jess—I won't step inside your circle.'

He was teasing, and I smiled, unsure what to say. After a long, waiting moment the fisherman rebaited his hook and flung his line out into the water, and I turned and walked back to my frolicking, leaping boys.

≈

That night, I lay in bed, scribbling in my notebook. After I discovered writing, I didn't feel the acute loneliness that had dogged me before. The things I couldn't say anywhere else felt said once I'd written them down. I wasn't writing journal entries but telling stories. If I recorded what had happened in narrative form, it existed somewhere outside of me.

For me, writing was all about secrets. Things unspoken, things unspeakable. I came to writing from a place of great isolation, and I wrote to tell secrets to myself. When my father took his life, colour leaked out of my world. Any aspirations I'd held for the future disappeared. My life felt full of holes. I lacked the opportunity to communicate what had gone wrong, and the space between me and everyone else seemed to swell, getting wider with every passing day. That is not to say that life didn't resume, because it did, but a concealed world opened up inside me, which, regardless of my external circumstances, remained hidden. I felt fractured, deeply. So when I started writing, it was not an act of sharing with others, but a kind of joining of my outside self with my hidden inside. An attempt at wholeness. A place where that lively self I had been in childhood could finally re-emerge. There was no reader. There was only me and me. I was whispering secrets in my own ear.

When you are invisible in your own world, you have zero standing. A shadow-walker, an outcast. You have reached a kind of bottom rung—you have nowhere to fall. There is a strange freedom in that nowhere space. When I wrote, I felt free from the shackles of judgment or shame or any sense of what I 'should' say, because I was already shunned. I wrote as though the world beyond the borders of my body wasn't even there. I wrote into the deepest silence. The power I felt in breaking that taboo—ploughing what had been an emotional wasteland—was monumental.

What I found most unexpected was what I uncovered. I'd been quiet so long, stored away so much, that I was like a cluttered cellar—all sorts of things were hidden in my depths. The thoughts–beliefs–images–people–emotions that I'd pushed away or denied were still swirling somewhere inside me, creating meanings and explanations that were often far beyond my conscious understanding. All sorts of mysterious things arose. I was writing about my life, yes. Things I believed wholeheartedly to be true. But I knew my stories were also a type of fiction, built on the fallibility of memories, and those mixed-up tales we tell.

'I'd like to read them,' Varda said, more than once.

It was hard to imagine sharing my words with another, but

when I plucked up enough courage, I left her a story to read after one of our sessions.

Once I was home, she rang me. 'I wouldn't normally do this,' she said hesitantly. 'Ring you without prior arrangement.'

I wondered what was wrong.

'It's just ... I read the story and ... I think ... I think it's something.'

I was dumbfounded, standing on the other end of the line.

'I'm not an expert,' she pushed on, 'but I believe your writing is of a publishable standard.'

'Really?'

'Jessie, I think you're a writer.'

≈

Living at the site of my trauma, I'd grown a thick skin. The garage where my father breathed his last breaths still stood, and I passed it daily on the way to my car. It seems inconceivable, but I rarely thought of him when I glanced inside. The garage had taken on a new purpose. We no longer parked there. My mother used it to store the fabrics she needed to make the cushions she sold at the markets. The space didn't haunt me, the way you might expect. Sometimes old friends of my father visited and I could see them brace themselves as they walked through the door, so overcome by the presence of the past that they could barely conceal their discomfort. His drawings still hung on the walls, and everything was much as he had left it.

'I don't know how you stand it,' Billie once said. But staying was two incongruous experiences at the same time: comforting yet sometimes also distressing. Home can be a complicated notion, the word itself conjuring all sorts of laden imagery. Put it beside 'family' and you've got a potent mix. From what I'd witnessed, most people ran as far from the site of their early trauma as they could, tripping over the debris in their haste. But I was like a fish swimming against the current, knocking again and again on the door of my childhood, wanting—somehow—to get back inside.

≈

Sometimes the house threw up a surprise that would take me unawares. Folding the washing, I got distracted by a book on the bookshelf and pulled it out. When I saw the single nail-hole through the top I sucked in a breath, the memory of my father's shrine splashing over me unexpectedly. Scattered through the many bookshelves, these novels were camouflaged, their spines unmarked. Plucking out a book, I never knew when I might find one. I stood there, holding the book in my palms as though within it might be some kind of answer. Smoothing my fingers along the cover and over the indented nail-hole, I randomly opened the pages. Like artefacts, these books were imbued with meaning: dense and historical. It was hard to know what to do with the feelings they aroused. The intensity of the memory had no place in my day-to-day life. Slipping the book carefully back between the others, I picked up the pile of clean clothes and took it into the bedroom.

Washing sorted, I was restless. The boys' voices were unceasing, and I retreated out to the trampoline to stretch out on my back and watch the sliding clouds. It was hot, and I could hear the buzz of nearby insects and the loud call and reply of the whipbirds. I peered up at the sky and then turned my face and watched the soft, springing movement of the palm fronds that curved into the skyscape.

Milla and Luca wandered outside sucking on ice-blocks my mother had made for them the night before. They were quiet except for the smacking of their lips against the orange ice. Standing close by, they kicked at the grass with their toes and then climbed up beside me on the trampoline.

'Don't drip those up here—it will be so sticky.' My words were a habit, offered routinely at the sight of a dripping ice-block, and the boys continued sucking without remark. Milla perched himself comfortably on the edge of the trampoline. I closed my eyes, and Luca leaned his back against the upright triangle of my knees.

'Mum, can we go somewhere today?' Milla asked, and though I didn't open my eyes, I knew how carefully he was watching me.

'Where would you like to go?'

'To the beach maybe. The hook beach. We could get fish and chips after.'

Nudging Luca aside, I turned over onto my belly.

'Maybe a bit later when it's not so hot,' I replied. The boys finished their ice-blocks and jumped down, throwing the plastic sticks into the garden.

'You better pick them up and put them in the sink, otherwise they'll get lost.'

Plucking the sticks from among the bromeliads, Milla and Luca ran back inside the house, and I could hear the oscillating tones of their game. The singsong to-and-fro of their words. Listening to my sons' voices, I pressed my face into the black weave of the trampoline mat. Through tiny squares of light I could see the patchy grass beneath. I watched the brown ant-mounds for signs of life.

In a moment the boys came running back, armed with scrap-books and textas.

'Nonny got them down for us. She said we could draw out here with you on the trampoline.' Milla's eyes were bright as he climbed up beside me. I sprang up and down as the trampoline mat adjusted to his weight.

'Okay, but no bouncing.'

Luca pulled himself up, opening his pencil case so that the coloured textas flowed out over the surface of the black mat and rolled towards me. If I jostled around to create some space for myself, the boys would just nudge in closer, filling it up. As he drew, Milla's tongue poked from his lips. He was careful, precise. In contrast, Luca drew endless smiling faces, just two dots and a curved-line mouth flung out from the end of his texta at high speed. In a few minutes he was bored and began to colour the metal springs of the trampoline. Milla drew on in silence, and Luca crawled off the edge and wandered back inside.

'What are you drawing?' I asked.

'A picture.'

I could hear the scratch of the texta against the paper.

'Of what?'

'It's a map.'

I turned my head to look over my shoulder at him. 'Hold it up for me.'

Milla drew one more line and then lifted the scrapbook to show me. Abstract oval lines and blocks of colour. I was always surprised by Milla's drawings.

'What's it a map of?'

'It's a map so no one ever gets lost. I'm going to roll it up and get a rubber band so it will be a … a … you know those things?'

I thought a minute, delving for the word.

'A scroll?'

'Yeah, a scroll, so no one ever gets lost.'

'That's pretty fancy,' I said, wondering who he worried might get lost.

'Mum, can I draw on you?'

'Where on me?'

Milla climbed carefully up on my back, a brown texta in his hand. He sat on me and bounced lightly and I smiled, my face turned to the side.

'Can I draw on your back, here?' Pressing his fingers softly into my shoulder, Milla rolled over to lie beside me.

'Just a little picture,' I murmured. 'Just one.'

Sitting up, he leaned forward and set to work. He was quiet and I closed my eyes.

'Finished,' he said after a minute or so.

'What did you draw?'

'Daddy. I drew Daddy on your back.'

I rolled over and looked at my oldest boy. 'You miss him?'

'Sometimes.'

'He'll come next Friday—you'll see him then.'

Milla nodded, turning his face away, and then smiled at me, a glancing, sideways smile.

'Can we go to the beach now, do you think?'

≈

I drove with the boys to the fisherman's beach. Milla and Luca rushed out of the car, their faces bright with recognition.

'It's the hook beach, Mum!'

Their voices swept towards me as they raced down to the water. I looked along the sand for the fisherman's silhouette, but the beach was deserted. An emptiness welled inside me at his absence, and I trailed after the boys down to the shore. They bounded about—tousled and playful—and I watched them with a secret longing. I envied my boys their freedom. They moved as though nothing pinned them down, no swamping dark history, no obdurate grief—as though they could at any time jump into the vast blue ocean and swim away, lively and free.

After a while I sat down at the shoreline, the ends of the waves washing up over my feet. My shadow stretched out before me on the sand, the sun low at my back.

'Jessie?'

The voice behind me was deep, and I knew it was him. The fisherman. I stood up quickly, trying to brush sand from my dress.

'Hi.'

He was the same, in his tatty fishing gear. The sun shone in my eyes, and I turned away from the glare, fighting the urge to cross my arms in front of my breasts.

'How you been?' he asked.

'Good.' I looked across at the boys.

'How's his finger?'

'It's fine. It just looked bad with the hook in it.'

The man watched my face, as if waiting for a sign. I could feel myself begin to blush, and I held up my hand to shield my eyes from his gaze. It shamed me that my body responded so overtly to his presence. He was silent and I moved to stand beside him with my back to the glare.

'How have you been?' It seemed a safe question.

'Yeah, all right.'

The boys spotted the fisherman and came wandering over, shells falling from their fingers. Sand encrusted, they smiled up at him from beneath their hats.

'Mum, do you know him?' Luca looked from me to the fisherman and back again.

I glanced at the fisherman's face and saw his quick smile.

'He's the man who got the hook out of your finger. Don't you remember?'

'I remember. But do you *know* him?'

'Well—' I realised that I'd never even asked the fisherman's name.

'I'm Sam.'

The man bent down and shook hands with Luca and then with Milla. Luca giggled, a bubbling, infectious laugh.

'What about Mum?'

Smiling, Sam held out his hand to me. Staring at the creases on his knuckles and the blunt curves of his nails, I willed myself to take it. Awkward, I squeezed his palm in my fingers, a tight, swift shake.

'There, now we're all friends.' Sam's voice was easy, as though the boys' presence had brought him a sudden lightness.

'Sam, come and see our castle.' Milla was excited, and I could see him trying to decide whether he should touch the fisherman's arm, his fingers lingering in midair. Sam moved towards the castle, turning to look at me as I followed. He crouched at the base of their odd-shaped creation and smoothed his palm across the top.

'What do you reckon, Jess—could this castle do with a tunnel through the middle?'

'Boys?' I knelt beside the fisherman on the sand. 'A tunnel through the middle?'

'Will it fall down?' Milla asked.

'No,' Sam said. 'There's a secret method. You boys start digging from that side, and I'll dig from this side. We'll meet in the middle, okay?'

As he pushed his fingers into the wall of the castle, Milla's face was sceptical. He scooped out a handful of sand, waiting to see if the castle would crumble. It held its shape, and Milla began to dig deeper inside. Luca stood watching.

'I think you're going to make it,' Luca piped up, always the optimist. He walked from one side to the other.

'Gotcha!' The fisherman smiled as he snagged Milla's fingers beneath the sand.

Lying on his belly, his arm stretched out inside the tunnel, Milla laughed and dropped his head, resting his cheek on the gritty beach. Sam pulled my son's fingers, making him giggle. I watched the man's smile, how the creases spread out from beside his eyes.

'Okay, let's look at this masterpiece.' Sam pulled his arm carefully from the tunnel of sand and sat back on his heels. Luca wandered back to me and flopped down into my lap, flicking off his wet hat.

'Looks good,' Sam said.

My smaller son sighed, peering up at the man beside him. Sam glanced between us, and I could see him searching for our resemblance. Leaning forward, I squeezed Luca in a tight embrace, hiding my face in his hair to escape scrutiny, but Luca wriggled and pulled his arms free.

'You have a little man drawn here.' Reaching out, Sam pointed at my back. He leaned towards me to get a proper look, and I tried not to tremble. My body seemed to find Sam's proximity unsettling. Dipping my face into Luca's damp curls again, I held my breath, forcing myself not to shift away.

'A tattoo?' Sam asked, glancing from Milla to Luca.

'I drew it,' Milla said, banging a hand down in the sand. 'It's my dad.' His face was suddenly pink and shuttered. 'He drinks too much and says fuck for nothing.'

Milla paused to take in the fisherman's response, but Sam was quiet.

'He doesn't wear his seatbelt,' Milla added, and the air shifted around us, a sharp, stinging breeze. I wanted to reach out an arm to my oldest son, to run a soothing hand along his shoulder, but I was pinned beneath Luca.

'Sweets, come here,' I said softly. 'I'll give you a cuddle.' But I knew he wouldn't.

I could feel the fisherman's gaze on me, but I didn't turn to face him.

'Can we go and get something to eat?' Milla collapsed crankily into the sand, knocking into the sandcastle.

'It's getting late, hey?' I nudged Luca from my knee and stood, brushing sand from my shins, avoiding the man's eyes.

Pulling Milla up, I drew both boys in against me.

'Sam, thanks for showing us your secret method,' I said, turning us all towards him.

'Bye, Sam—we're going now,' Luca said.

'Bye, Sam,' Milla whispered, looking down at the sand.

Lifting my arm over Luca's head, I held out my hand for Sam to shake, my self-consciousness suddenly gone. The boys wrapped their arms about my hips and I laughed as they pulled me away from the fisherman's touch and up towards the car.

'Mummy, you made a friend!' Luca's voice was high and questioning, and he looked sideways at me as I tried to remember where I'd stashed the keys.

'Yes. Sam. The fisherman.' I looked back at the beach with a surge of hope.

Sam lifted his arm and waved.

≈

In hindsight, it seems odd that I would experience such a sense of triumph in making a single friend—that a random guy snagging my son's finger with a fishhook would come to mean so much. Perhaps it was a good indication of the depth of my isolation. I latched on to the idea of him, the fisherman, as though he had caught me with his hook. But what I liked about Sam, right from the outset, was the way he didn't look away from me. It made me visible, where I had felt myself not to be. The power of the smallest kindnesses. In his unwavering gaze I came into the light.

That night, beneath the cover of darkness, I dreamed I was at the beach and lay naked on the sand with the fisherman. I lay on my side, my back to him and my cheek rested on the soft skin of my upper arm. I stared at the infinite white before me. The fisherman reached out and laid his palm on the curve of my shoulder.

'Trace the lines of my back and tell me what you see,' I whispered.

Motionless on the blanket of sand, I felt the touch of his fingertips across my back. In murmurs, the fisherman spoke of the sloping of my shoulders. He told me of the shallow hollow that ran straight down the centre of my back. His fingers drifted, and he traced the lines of the stretch marks that edged around from my hips. He spoke of the feel of my skin beneath his fingers. Meandering along an invisible path from dark freckle to dark freckle, he whispered to me of the exact point at which they each lay, and in my dream I closed my eyes and pictured the shadowy landscape of my own body, the parts of myself that I had never really seen. Lying still, his low voice filling my ears, I could feel the strong beating of my own heart.

When I woke the light was low. Curled up on my side, I thought of the curves and hollows of my back, the freckles and paler skin along my ribs. The room slowly brightened into day, and an image made up of this man's whispered dream-words formed inside my mind. I had been wounded, bent out of shape, but I was coming back together. Wrapping my arms about myself, I grasped gently at my shoulders. My skin was smooth and cool and firm beneath my fingertips.

≈

Living in the forest almost all of my life, there were some things I'd learned. I knew how to be still and listen. I could saw down the odd branch, tell what bush-fruit was edible. I often knew when it would rain, or if a storm was coming. I could step over a python without batting an eyelid. I didn't get frightened by spiders, bats, toads or wasps. I could catch a frog if it got tangled in spider webs. I could pump up water from the creek, get the air bubbles out of the pipes. I was exceptionally good at lighting a fire. Then there were all those things we'd always done for pleasure. I could swing off a rope at the waterhole, ride the creeks on a bodyboard in a flood, jump from bridges into the river, float for hours in a pond, tread barefoot up a mountain. These things might not be all that useful out in the world, but they are skills, and I had them.

But at twenty-five, with two kids under six, I was yet to learn very much about my own romantic proclivities. With just the one relationship under my belt, I hadn't had much chance to test those waters. Since Gabe's departure I'd come to see myself as not romantically inclined, or perhaps just not 'a romantic'.

When I'd told Billie I was separating from Gabe, she had tried to be upbeat.

'Well, it gives you a chance to meet someone else.'

'I don't know if that will happen,' I'd answered.

'It's not a matter of *if*,' she'd said confidently, 'but *when*.'

I'd loved her fiercely in that moment, for being so sure.

But until you test those waters, you can't know how you'll be. It turned out I had a rampant romantic imagination that fed off the tiniest titbits, blooming wildly with the minutest encouragement. It took me some time to work out that I was not the pragmatic type at all. It was rare for me to happen upon someone I liked, but when I did, the sheer force of my feelings seemed uncontainable. And with that discomfiting discovery came others. It was in romance that all my woundedness surfaced. Where the word 'trust' came to have such a dark, complex shadow. I didn't fear infidelity the way some people did. I was paralysed with fright over things trickier to determine. Would this person start off one way and then fundamentally change? Would they, if stretched to breaking point, lose their capacity to love me? Lose their mind? Would they, when push came to shove, abandon me in some final crazed act? In romance, everything felt slippery to me—there was nothing to grip on to. But at twenty-five, when I first met the fisherman, I was unaware of these dark fears. I was wary, yes, unused to company, and afraid no one would be able to bear the weight of my history. But I hadn't yet experienced myself as a wounded adult in love. That was all still to come.

≈

'How come you never bring your kids down here?' I asked, looking sideways at the fisherman, a cautious glance.

At the hook beach I sat on the sand above the waterline. He sat beside me, the sleeves of his green flannelette shirt rolled up past his elbows. I watched his hands as he scooped up the dry sand and slowly released it from inside his closed fists, making tiny pyramids at his feet.

'They're big now. Teenagers.' He paused, patting the pyramids flat. 'Sometimes they come down for a dip, after school, when it's real hot.'

I added that information to the image of him I was building in my mind.

'They used to love coming fishing with me. After my wife took off I used to bring 'em here every day. Stopped me going mad.'

I'd been wondering about his wife. Whether or not he had one.

'When did your wife leave?'

'Years ago now. The kids were little, littler than yours.'

'They still see her?'

'Nah, she took off to Darwin. Some other fella.'

'They must miss her.'

'I guess. Sometimes she rings, but they don't really want to talk.'

'Do they talk with you?' It was easy to ask him questions, deflect things from me.

'Nah, they won't talk about the big stuff.' He looked out to sea. 'Sometimes I try, but they won't really listen.'

'What would you want to tell them?'

It was hard to imagine my sons all grown up.

'It's not telling them, it's just talking. I try, but they just look at me like it's not what they're after. Like I'm off the mark,' he sighed. 'She's got another family now, with a couple of little kids. Sometimes I wonder what she tells them.'

'About your kids?'

'Nah, none of that. The type of stuff she might talk to our kids about if she was still around—if she'd never left, you know?'

He didn't sound bitter.

'Do you miss her?'

Sam looked across at me, his eyes dark but faintly smiling. 'It's hard to live with someone unhappy, and she was always unhappy with me.' He shrugged. 'I guess I just wonder how it might have been.'

How it might have been. The age-old question.

'We had this bookshelf in our room,' he said, 'all her girly books. And when she first started acting strange I used to lie in bed and stare at those books, sometimes all night.'

I knew all about sleeplessness.

'When she took off, she left them,' he said. 'I got curious, picked one up and started to read. I read the lot of them in a couple of weeks. It was like being able to live in another world. Bitchy boardroom slags, you know? The rich and famous. You ever read any?'

'Yeah. I've read some.' I pushed my fingers into the sand.

He looked at my face. 'I thought they'd help me make sense of her, but they just got me thinking instead. All that time my wife had been reading those books and I didn't know what kind of world she was living in.' He smiled, a little sadly. 'Like all the real living we'd done, it was on the outside, and on the inside she'd had this other place I'd never even been to. I started to feel like I hadn't known her at all.' His fingers curled into a soft fist.

'And it wasn't just the books. She had a whole other life.'

'People are mysterious. You can't live inside another person's head.'

I thought of Zoe's letters home, how little they revealed of her inner landscape. How we'd never known what was going on. Picking up a handful of sand, I reached out, trickling it slowly over Sam's fist. He stretched his fingers out and I watched the fine white flecks nestle in between the dark hairs.

'I know. But I didn't know it then.' He stared back out at the ocean and I wondered what he was thinking.

'Where are the boys today?' he asked.

'With their dad. He takes them sometimes for a day on the weekend.'

'They like it?'

'Yeah, Gabe's reformed nowadays. Not so much drinking.' I wasn't sure how much to say. 'It's funny how some people only seem to learn by losing something.'

Sam kept staring out to sea. 'Yeah … me too, I guess.'

I hadn't meant to draw this parallel, but now it sat there between us. I leaned forward, smoothing a spiral in the sand with my finger.

'I'm sorry about your wife, Sam.' I was struggling to speak coherently. 'Sometimes the lesson is way harder than it should be.' Trying not to mumble. 'Irreparable. Irrecoverable. I know that.'

'How do you know, Jess?' His voice was quiet, sad. Like he already knew it was something bad.

Pulling my knees up, I wrapped my arms tightly about them. Sharing the facts never ended well. I wanted to reveal something to this man, but I knew how this went. I was afraid of Sam's silence, of his withdrawal from me, and at the same time I was afraid of his words, of what he might say. Trust was a fragile thing.

'Jess?'

'It's not a good story.'

'You don't want to tell it?'

Sam lifted a handful of sand and spilled it slowly over my arm. A pyramid built in the crease of my elbow, and when there was no more sand left Sam flattened it and gently rubbed the particles away. His touch was light, and I felt something inside me release.

Be brave, I told myself. *Try again.*

'My sister committed suicide when I was twelve.' The words came fast. 'It seemed an unbearable lesson to learn. Her lesson to us.' Short and sharp. 'Irreparable. Irrecoverable. My father couldn't salvage himself.' I sucked in a breath. 'He died six years later.'

'How?'

'He killed himself too.'

'How'd he do it?'

'In the car. I mean, he tried to slit his wrists first, but it didn't work.'

'How old was your sister?'

'Eighteen.'

'How'd she do it?'

'Gas too, from an oven. In Holland. She was travelling.'

'Why'd she do it?'

I looked across at the fisherman, his hands loose, relaxed between his knees. The unanswerable question.

'Unspeakable sadness, I guess.' I shrugged. 'Why does anyone choose to die?'

In my reckoning, experience wasn't as simple as points on a map, leading in a clear direction, though we were narrative-hungry creatures, and tended to think it so. We all tried to make sense of the present by looking at the past, but I was beginning to see that every moment was fresh, and each of us—in any given minute—might take multiple different paths. There was *always* the life we lived and the life we could have lived, if only we'd chosen differently. I didn't believe Zoe had to die that day. There were other roads she could have walked.

'Sometimes I think if she'd just lived through that day, maybe she wouldn't have done it. Maybe she just needed one more day.'

He reached out, like he was going to wrap his arm around me, and I tensed, my heart beating against my chest, an ancient flight mechanism setting in. Sam dropped his hand, tilting his head to watch me.

'I won't touch you, Jess,' he said softly. 'I can see how stiff you go when you think I might touch you.'

I'm a prickly thing, Sam.

I don't know how I got this way.

I tasted tears in my mouth, but I gritted my teeth against them.

'I wasn't always like this,' I whispered. 'I don't know how to *be.*'

Sam shifted around, kneeling on the beach in his fisherman jeans. He scooped up a mound of fine sand, trailing it slowly from inside his hands, and I watched the graceful glide of white.

'You've been hurt, Jess. Sometimes that makes us—' He grappled with words.

'Prickly?'

'Yeah … I mean … it can.'

'But I've never been hurt in that way. Never … physically. Half the hurts I carry around aren't even mine.'

Sand slid from hand to hand, a shuffling motion, smooth and rhythmic.

'It doesn't matter whose.'

I held out my arm, and Sam scattered a delicate line down my bare forearm, elbow to fingertips and back again. I quivered a little and the sand dropped away. Reaching out, he repeated the uneven sliding line. This time I was utterly still, watching the fall of sand, balancing it, letting it build into small pyramids.

'My mum used to sprinkle me like this when I was little.' I felt myself sigh. 'I'd lie down on my belly and she'd sprinkle me with sand,' I added. 'It feels tickly and nice. The sand's cool in the afternoon.'

Sam paused, watching me.

'I could sprinkle you,' he said, picking up a handful of sand.

I hadn't known this physicality would be so hard for me. As a child I'd been free with my body—affection had been easily given and received. Here on the beach, I could sense Sam's

219

kindness. In my dream world I had craved his touch. With my rational mind, I knew Sam was no threat, but my body was on red alert. Poised for flight, in panic mode. I wondered if it was a response to trauma, this heightened hypervigilance. I suspected Varda would know.

'Close your eyes, then I'll lie down,' I said softly, hoping my body would oblige.

Sam knelt in the sand, his eyes closed, arms hanging by his sides. I turned onto my belly.

'You ready?' he asked.

'Yeah.'

Opening his eyes, Sam smiled and I laughed in reply, a sighing giggle. My cheek rested against the fine white sand.

'Do you need something for a pillow?'

Sam began to take off his flannelette shirt, but I shook my head. 'I'm okay. Just start.'

Slowly, I inched my forearms out from beneath my sides. Like a turtle I had folded myself away and now I cautiously unfurled my limbs. Trying to still my racing heartbeat, I looked out past the fisherman and along the stretch of beach before my eyes. Sam moved around me on his knees, scooping up sand and trailing it slowly along my shoulder and down my arm. Delicate and soothing, the sand sprinkled in fine lines over each curving finger. I focused on the minute specks before my eyes, the waves beyond a distant blur.

The fisherman traced the length of my calves poking from beneath my skirt. Softly the sand slid from his fingers, an unhurried arc of white, and Sam shuffled down and released a light trickle onto my feet. Settling between my toes, it tickled, and I couldn't help but squirm. Sam scooped up another handful and buried my wiggling feet completely.

'Too ticklish?' His voice seemed to come from far away, and I sat up abruptly, sand sliding from me in a glittering fall. Exposed and tingling, I fought the urge to run.

'No, it was good. Your turn.'

'You sure?'

'Yeah.'

Sam lay down slowly on the sand, closing his eyes. I could see his breath ease out in a long sigh, his body all softness. I watched him a moment before I cupped a handful of sand. His arms drifted out from his body, his hands curled like seashells against the white. Leaning over, I surveyed the arc of his fingers, trickling sand down his forefinger, curving around to his thumb. Then, taking small pinches, I sprinkled his knuckles, and filled the space between his fingers with soft rows of sand until tiny walls grew up enclosing them. He was motionless. The sand blew against his eyelids in speckled dots. He looked so vulnerable, lying there, and everything seemed so fleeting.

'Sam?'

'Hmm?'

'I'm just going to get something. Don't move, I'll come back.'

I stood and walked down to the breaking waves. Rocks and shells lay washed up on the shoreline, broken but smooth, and I leaned down and scooped them into my singlet. I was indiscriminate in my choosing, picking up everything I could see.

Walking back up towards him, I emptied my singlet onto the sand in a cacophony of sudden sound. Kneeling, I sorted quickly through the pebbles and shells. With quick, darting movements I arranged the rocks around Sam's sandy fist. I placed the shells—pipi-shaped and smooth—in the sand around his head. Wisps of his hair wafted against my fingers and I glanced down at his eyes, but they were closed. He was unmoving, as though sleeping.

I outlined his shape with my jumbled collection, pushing the shells lightly downwards with my thumb. With no shells left, I walked back to the shoreline to collect more, and returning, released them at Sam's feet in a scattering slide. I placed them against his feet and calves, and when I'd arranged the shells and pebbles in a vague silhouette, I crawled across to kneel at his side, his sand-encrusted hand at my knees.

'You can move now—I'm finished,' I whispered.

Sam's speckled eyelids opened and he gazed up at me, for a moment unseeing.

'Were you really asleep?' I felt suddenly like laughing. 'Move carefully.'

Sam raised his head, looking over his shoulder at the shells and rocks.

'You've made me in the sand.'

'Yep.'

Gingerly, he lifted his body up, trying not to disturb the silhouette of shells and rocks. He dusted the sand from his clothes and smiled sideways at me, his cheek white with a fine veil of particles that crumbled and fell away with his grin.

'It's beautiful, Jess.'

'Mmm. Your imprint.'

'Wonder how long it'll last,' he said.

'It's above the waterline—it won't get washed away.'

'Some dog might come past and dig it up.'

'Or some wild kids like mine.'

'A surfer might dump his gear here without even looking.'

I turned towards him, my restless fingers hidden beneath the hem of my singlet.

'Maybe the wind will just blow it all away.'

Sam watched my face, and I stared across the sand to my car, wordless, the magnetic pull of home suddenly upon me.

'Time to go?' He stepped back, as though to let me pass.

'Do you ever come here early for the sunrise?' I asked.

'Sometimes.'

'Must be beautiful, hey? You can't see the sky at my house.'

'Why? You live in a cave?'

Glancing back towards him, I laughed. 'No. It's beautiful, my place, but there are so many trees. You can't see the sky, not like this, just pockets here and there. Small pockets of blue. No sunsets. No sunrises. I can see the moon, though, when it's full, from my bedroom window.'

'Does it keep you awake?'

I looked up at the broad expanse of the sky. 'I'm not a good sleeper. I get restless, moon or no moon. But I like to see it. I feel

223

connected in some way. It's silly—I mean, it's just the moon, right?'

'Jess?'

'Yeah?'

'I'm sorry about your sister, and your dad.' He spoke slowly, like there was no hurry. 'I thought you must have had something real sad happen. Something about you—'

I wondered if I was marked, if all my hurts were visible in some way, but I didn't want to ask. The afternoon had moved towards night and I could see the shadow of the evening upon my skin. A glittering kind of darkness.

'Sam?'

'Yeah?'

'You'll be here, won't you, if I come back? Another day. You won't just disappear?'

'Blown away by the wind?'

'Yeah.'

The dimming sky seemed all at once to close in, and I looked away from Sam's face, downwards, smoothing my foot through the sand in a wide arc.

'I've been here a while, Jess. I'll be here a while yet.'

≈

At my next session with Varda, I told her about the fisherman and my recalcitrant body. She was thoughtful for a long moment.

'It's a common experience for trauma survivors to have

problems with intimacy,' she said finally.

I thought about an old primary school friend of my brother's, about how I'd bumped into him recently and he'd stood there, awkwardly, asking, 'Is it okay to hug you?' I'd laughed, and he'd looked at me carefully. 'Oh, it's only that when I last saw you, you said you don't do touch.' Demonstrating, he'd held up his palms, as though warding me off.

I'd been shocked. 'When did I say that?'

'Last time I saw you, just after your father died.'

I'd had no memory of it. No memory at all.

In the studio now with Varda, I stammered, 'But I never had any trouble like that with Gabe.'

I wondered about my withdrawal from Gabe. I'd always thought it began when I first got pregnant, but maybe it was earlier.

'Trouble with sex? Or trouble with intimacy?' Varda asked, watching my face.

'Sex,' I answered hesitantly. 'It was probably the thing we did best.' I wasn't sure about intimacy. We'd been good at it once.

She nodded. 'Well, historically speaking, you'd always seen him as a safe place. Probably he didn't set off any fight or flight impulses.'

'And the fisherman does?'

I could see Varda was thinking.

'Well, excitement and fear have very similar bodily sensations,' she said. 'Racing heartbeat, heightened perception, tingling. Sometimes, when there's been a big shock, your nervous system gets the two things scrambled, like wires crossed.'

This was alarming.

'But how do I overcome it?'

'We can come up with some strategies.' She smiled. 'But, basically, you've just got to try to take things slow.'

≈

In grief, denial has its own adaptive purpose. We stay there until we are ready or able to feel the pain. The commonly identified stages of grief—denial, anger, bargaining, depression, acceptance—are only a loose guide. Many of us step off the beaten track. What pushes us from one state to the other is mysterious, though we might like the process to follow a neat narrative line. Possibly there are unconscious mechanisms at work. We dream, and over time some of these messier feelings get disentangled in our sleep.

I didn't know why I had refused for so long to read the ripped-up letter my father had sent me in the months before he died. Perhaps in my anger I didn't have any space for his suffering. When someone takes their own life it is hard to forget that they have chosen to leave you. That whatever love they had for you wasn't enough to make them stay. They didn't just move interstate, or across the world—they left you forever. And even if you know their pain was unbearable, deep down you will always wonder if it was because you weren't worth sticking around for. You didn't, in the end, make life worth living. Knowing what my father had wanted to tell me in those last months had always been more than I could bear, but with Varda in my life I knew I wouldn't have to shoulder all the weight.

Gathering the shovel, scissors, camera, sticky tape and glue, all possibilities covered, I descended the ridge to my special place out past the clothes line. Out of sight of my mother, I made my way down the red mud slope, through the barbed wire and across the creek. On the higher ground the curved stick sagged from its hole, marking the burial spot. Milla and Luca were with Gabe, and without them I had come to dig up the past, to uncover my metal box with its hidden letter, torn and maimed.

The dirt was soft, and I leaned the shovel against a tree and scraped at the small mound with my fingers. The layer underneath was damp and the soil came away in easy handfuls. In the shortest time I saw the glint of metal. Smoothing away the clinging dirt, I pried open the box and stared for a moment at the creased envelope inside.

The letter from him.

This time, I was ready to read it.

Settling on a dry, flat spot, I scraped aside the leaves, clearing the way, and tipped up the envelope, watching as the scraps of white paper fluttered to the ground. The messy ink-scrawl of my father's handwriting glared at me from the hard dirt, but I wanted to piece the letter together first and try to absorb its meaning later. As I inspected the writing for connections and began the puzzle of his words, I hummed a tune, the sound of the song soothing. I worked, arranging the words, and then sticking them down when they fitted properly.

The letter appeared slowly before my eyes, stuck straight against the dirt with a white drop of glue. One page complete. Two pages complete. I cleared away more leaves, needing space to finish the rest. Three pages, four. My neck ached as I crouched before the scraps of paper, but I was becoming expert now at seeing the way my father's words fitted together. I looked away for a moment to get my bearings. The creek murmured beside me, reflective and shady. I watched the water swirl across the rocks. Close to finishing the last page, tears slipped from my eyes, smudging the seven-year-old ink.

It was hard not to read the words as they appeared. I listened to the rushing of the water, focusing on the sounds around me, wrenching my mind away from thoughts of my father, until finally it was all done.

Not yet. Not quite yet.

I looked away from the finished puzzle, standing aside and walking across to the water. Tucking up my skirt, I stepped in, watching as the rapids raced around my ankles. I breathed—a deep pull of air—then exhaled, leaning forward to dip my fingertips beneath the gushing coolness. The water was fresh and soft against my fingers, and I picked up a stray leaf and sent it careering down the flowing current, watching it disappear beyond my sight.

After a minute or so, I moved from the water towards the white map of my father's words. Kneeling before the letters, I began at last to read.

March 12

Dear Jess

LETTER WRITING

—Personal, that is. I was sitting here thinking about this. It's a pretty odd sort of thing.

THOUGHTS

1. *Once there was a time when letter writing was the only form of communication.*

2. *Who to?*

3. *How often?*

4. *How long?*

5. *What's in it?*

6. *What is the connection between the written & spoken word?*

7. *What do you censor?*

8. *Is it actually a kind of love affair on paper?*

9. *100 other things.*

10. *Some people write heaps, others none. Why?*

11. *Maybe it gets boring?*

12. *Maybe you repeat yourself because you forget what you said last time.*

13. *What space to devote to perusing the last letter & maybe responding to things in that?*

14. *Half of 'Possession' which I've got here is letter writing. (A.S. Byatt (female) set partly around 1860.)*

15. *There were lots of other things going around in my head about this subject but they've disappeared temporarily.*

16. *Have you got lousy writing, so you miss too many words— maybe even 10 missed words in a page is too many?*

17. *'Possession' is a pretty amazing book filled with lots of letters from 1860s, the letters intensify—it's a 500 page book. Sometimes their letters—being so Victorian—drove me crazy—I preferred the current story—and they swapped poems too—lots—(not my scene). But it is also about two people researching these people now. I think I'll read it again, starting tomorrow.*

18. *I think I mentioned that it hurts my hand to write—is my body telling me something? Is it saying—<u>well don't!</u> Or is it just arthritis (which it is on x-ray).*

19. *Is it therapy? (Yes)—mutual, or just self therapy? Depends I guess.*

20. *My letters (this kind) are always night-time ones, usually after alcohol, and sometimes end at 3 am. They gather momentum probably become more disorganised—a real adrenaline buzz.*

21. *Your mum is an absolute non-letter writer—(or card sender)—not her style at all. My mother used to write (very briefly). Would always end (except once) with 'well son, I suppose I should close (after 2 minutes) because I've got to go shopping' or something … I forget.*

22. *What do you do with the letters after you've read them, especially if a lot of effort has gone into them?*

When you sat down and went blank, I think it's just that you thought—what the hell am I going to write here? Head full of thoughts, ideas, emotions, but just what to say? Tentativeness enters. Will this upset the other person? Do I really want to write this?

ANOTHER MAD TOPIC

Manics just about universally are letter writers, and they write much more when manic. (I'm not manic.) That phenomenon is pretty amazing because it's just about <u>diagnostic</u>. But—they're (we're) letter writers <u>anyway</u>. (Not when depressed.) Then later super intense!!!

End of part 1.
Love Dad

≈

March 25
(13 days later)

Dear Jess

IN RESPONSE TO YOUR LETTER:

1. *I never knew that I made you so angry for so long. Certainly after '94 I did, but not before. (Remember no answers are required.)*

2. *There's pre/post manic time. I know post manic time was a disaster, but didn't think my behaviour was so bad pre-'94.*

3. *Lot of 'I didn't know'(s) in here. But that's the way it is.*

4. *Zoe's childhood was very different. Marriage break-up age 2, and chronically super-smart elder sister. (And Zoe's mother was a lot like Zoe. In for instance the violence of their poetry & dancing. Both amazing dancers & savage black poets.)*

5. *Childhood—Janny's total unconditional love certainly worked. I think she just learnt that from her mother or parents. My childhood love (I can't remember any). My upbringing was based on punishment and no rewards so I learnt all that. Mind you, Janny is one of the most perfect mothers in existence.*

6. *When I went mad in '94 I self mutilated in various ways. The most obvious was the mandalas in my palms. But I <u>thought</u> I outstared the sun (for about 2 minutes)—my timing was off—obviously. It seemed like I'd beat it, and kept on staring. I was rather proud of the mandalas cut into my palms (with cracked mirror) but everything else was rubbish.*

7. *<u>You said in your letter that you had</u>: 'A general worry about <u>you</u> or your effect on mum'. Well it's best to be honest. It's not very reassuring, but it happened, that's me. I don't want to make a story up about anything. (There are tactful omissions but that's not really my scene.)*

I know that during the peace following August/Sept/Oct '95, when you guys moved to the yellow house, Janny has got tearful when I've been there. I notice you both (you and Jake) notice & are very protective, and I think—'Shit, it will be seen as my fault again.' But I don't think it necessarily is, it's just that I'm <u>there</u> and some little thing (or bigger thing) comes up about the present—eg. Property Settlement, or something 10 years ago. And Janny cries and I don't, and you guys think 'this arsehole is still at it'.

Dunno if this letter is going in quite the right direction. But I love your mother and I know that she just tolerates me and that hurts me all the time. And before long she'll meet someone who loves her, and that worries me. I know it will happen because she's so beautiful physically & mentally (nearly) and then I'm gone and without hope.

8. *'Listening?' Dunno. I can't think of any good qualities I possess.*

9. *'Did I love Zoe best?' I don't know. She/Me were the great nightmare. She was vastly the most difficult for me. But we never really got on. Well with a mother like Janny, you two were obviously safe, and Billie was always self-sufficient.*

10. *It's very hard to know with a scenario of:*
    Billie 16—self-sufficient
    Zoe 14—wild & emotional (and in special need)
    You 7—with a proper mummy & super cute (sorry)
    Jake 5—the boy.

11. *I think you underestimate what I 'notice'.*

My drinking and smoking is a form of slow self-destruction. It's a bad part of my personality that's probably always been there. Zoe's death certainly didn't help at all because I still feel the pain of some responsibility for her action, in several different ways.

Today has been a black pit day. Sometimes there are grey pits. Sometimes even normal days (nearly).

Maybe I contributed something to you. It took me 50 years to realise that my father contributed a lot more than I ever thought.

It was a lovely letter you wrote.

My greatest loss is Janny, because I don't think I've really lost you or Jake.

I do love you.

(And admire and respect you.)

Hardly anyone feels this way about me. I am a liability, a
burden and an embarrassment. (For me more than anyone else.)
I think I used to be something but I've forgotten those times.
Love Dad

≈

I leaned over the pages, dripping tears, letting my father's pain wash over me. I imagined him alone at the kitchen table, drunk, writing those words. My father had striven—always—to be exactly who he was, but even so I was shocked by his honesty. I thought about how he had chosen to live as though his own childhood didn't exist—how, despite my curiosity, I'd never learned anything concrete about it. His description so stark: *My childhood love (I can't remember any).*

How hard he had tried to break that pattern of punishment and no rewards. The love for me he had always expressed, sitting in the letter, captured there in time. But his suffering, overwhelming everything. If I'd read the letter at the time he sent it, would I have known what he was planning? Probably not. Before his death, I had never believed that he would leave me. Despite all his madness, despite the fact I knew he threatened it, I had trusted him to stay. I thought of the note he left, scrawled out beside him in the car.

Billie, Jessie, Jakey—I'm sorry.

Short and to the point. Apologising for what he knew to be the deepest betrayal—that his love for us, in those final moments, could not overcome his pain.

'I'm sorry too,' I whispered and, crouching beside the letter, I felt myself begin to rock. How hard it was to truly hear another's sorrow. My heart hurt beneath my ribs and I pressed my fingers into the pain. Minutes passed, long and slow.

Standing, I turned away from my father's words and walked back to the creek. Stepping into the shallow centre, I lowered myself into the water. I let it flow over me, pulling at my clothes and heavy, streaming hair. It was cold and the rocks against my back were hard. Lying in the chilly water, the bouncing tinkle of it was lost to my submerged ears. I closed my eyes to the canopy of leaves overhead, pushing my head back to let the creek pour across my face. It was dark and quiet inside my mind, and I held my breath and felt the silky movement of the current around me.

I imagined my father's sad words being prised from inside me and surging away down the rushing creek. In my mind I watched as the words curved around the bend below me and disappeared into the jostling waters downstream. I saw them meander along the passage of the winding creek until they joined a river and plunged on towards the sea. In the ocean, the words were sucked towards the horizon. In the ploughing of waves they began to disintegrate—letters pulled from letters—until the dismembered vowels and consonants floated about, detached and drifting.

I came up for air with a gasp, then lay still in the water, watching the sway of the towering branches above, waiting for the next leaf to drop. Cold, I sat up, my clothes sticking to me, smothering and tight. I rose from the creek, wringing water from my skirt. Flicking my hands dry, I picked up my camera and photographed each page. This push and pull, always: to let go, to hold on. I didn't want the letter anymore, but I didn't want there to be no record of it either, and I wanted to be able to show it to Varda if I needed to. I gathered up the supplies I had brought, then—averting my eyes from the pages of my father's letters—pulled myself, still dripping, back through the barbed wire and up the sliding slope.

≈

That afternoon, Jake arrived with Gemma for the night, and I hung back, giving him space. Settling into the couch, he sat, guitar on lap, sipping tea. My mother had gone to the shops, and it was just us, the three of us.

Gemma was in the kitchen looking at recipe books.

'Jake?' I perched on the edge of a chair, trying to figure out how to broach the subject. That chasm that lay between us, the thing we never spoke of.

'Yeah?'

'I read this letter today. A letter from Dad. I hadn't ever read it before.'

Jake stilled, as though frozen mid-movement.

'He sent me this letter after I left home, but he tore it up before he put it in the post, so it arrived in pieces. I wouldn't read it then, but I kept it, you know, in the envelope.' I was finding it hard to explain. 'When he died, I just couldn't bear it. I couldn't make myself read it.'

I rolled up the hem of my singlet with trembling hands.

'What did it say?' Jake looked down at the carpet, away from my face. I could hear Gemma clanking dishes in the kitchen.

'It was Dad being Dad. Lists of things, and a bit of a rave about the book *Possession*. It was an answer to a letter I'd written him. But it was sad, really sad. He was very low, broken. He said he loved me, but he always said that.'

'Can I read it?'

'Are you sure you want to?' I didn't want to cause my brother any more pain.

Glancing back towards the kitchen, Jake nodded.

'Well, it's down there,' I pointed. 'Down the ridge, beside the creek. Where we used to play.'

Together we crossed the grass to the clothes line, walking over the brown ant-mounds to the slope. I climbed down first, and at the bottom I held the barbed wire apart for Jake to slide through, wincing as his shirt caught against a hard spike. Jake slipped off his shoes, leaving them on the bank, and stepped through the water.

'It's there. On the ground. I stuck it down with glue.'

I did not want to see the black ink-scrawl again, and I wavered on the other side of the bank, watching. My heartbeat quickened. Jake squatted, leaning his weight against his fingertips, and I watched him lift his hand to swipe at his eyes. He read slowly, and I stood across the water, holding my breath.

Finally Jake turned to me, eyes red and swollen. 'It's not your fault, you know, Jess. The not reading it.'

'I know.' I sucked in a breath. 'It's just sad. Even if I'd read it then, it probably would have just made me angry.'

Jake stood and wandered to the creek edge. 'You weren't there when he died. You were with Billie in Japan.'

'Yes, I was gone.'

'I never told you what happened the night before.'

My brother's words propelled me forward and I stepped through the barbed-wire fence.

'No, you never told me.'

'Dad was over at our place, the cottage down at the beach, and he was stomping around, ranting about something, like he always did. Mum and I were lying on the couch, just lying there while he yelled and yelled, and then I said, "Dad, no one cares."'

My brother peered down at the flowing water.

'He stopped ranting. He just stood still in the middle of the room. I'd never said anything like that before.' My brother turned from me, wandering back towards our father's words. 'He was silent for a minute, and then he said, "No one cares?" And Jess, I said it again. He looked kind of stunned, and then he turned around and walked out.'

Crossing the creek, I drifted over to where Jake crouched beside our father's letter.

'But Jake, they're just words, right? You know it's not your fault?'

'I know. But it's like all those years that he was bad and you and Mum would get angry and I never said anything. And on that day I'd just had enough, and I finally spoke, and I knew as soon as the words were out that they were wrong, and then I said them again.'

Watching tears slide from my brother's eyes, I squatted on the ground beside him.

'In the morning when I got up, I was upset about it, and Mum told me that after I'd gone to bed she'd rung Dad up, and that they'd talked for ages, and that he'd understood that I didn't mean it. That she'd known I was worried, and so she'd rung. Mum told me Dad was okay about it.' He paused, sighing. 'But when he wouldn't answer his phone, I just knew.' Jake kept his eyes on the ground. 'Mum wouldn't let me come with her to the house, but it didn't matter—I knew he was dead.'

I reached out my hand to touch my brother. His body trembled beneath my palm.

'The worst thing is, it occurred to me a few years later that maybe Mum didn't make that phone call.' His voice clogged up. 'Maybe she never spoke to him that night—maybe she just didn't want me to feel bad, and so she said she did.'

Creeping towards my brother, I wrapped my arms around him while he cried. I shook my head, wanting to deny his words, wanting to catch them all up and float them all away.

'But Jake, it's not your fault,' I whispered. 'Dad was so awful— you were allowed to get mad.'

Jake's body was soft, his face turned away.

'But Jess, I never said anything to him. It was the only time I ever spoke.'

I cried then too, soft, gulping sobs, holding tight to my grown-up younger brother.

'Let's wash it all away.' I pointed to the letter stuck down on the dirt. 'Let's pick it off, and float it downstream.'

'Do you want to?'

'Yeah. Let's.'

'Okay.'

I scratched at the paper, tearing it off the earth, and the puzzle of my father's words came away in my hands. Jake reached out and pulled at the torn edges. With a handful each we walked back to the creek. I dropped the first scrap and, fluttering down, it landed on the water, tumbling away quickly downstream. Waiting, I watched as Jake plucked a thin white fragment from his hand and released it to the transparent slide of the water.

'Okay, now more,' I said as I opened my palms.

Throwing the shreds into the air, I watched them spiral downwards, sucked away in a sudden gush as they landed. Jake glanced across at me with a wobbly smile and then emptied his white scraps into the creek.

'I'll get the rest.' He turned back to scrape up more of our father's words. I watched him from the creek edge, hoping that I was right to speak, right to tell Jake of the letter, right to bring him down to see it.

Jake stepped towards me, holding out his hand.

'Do you want to, Jess?'

'No, you do it.'

He scattered the remnants of the letter, and it rushed down-stream, disappearing beneath the surface of the water.

'Jess?'

'Yeah?'

'I always wanted to tell you what I said.'

≈

Up at the house, I could see Gemma take note of Jake's red eyes.

'I'll make tea,' she said simply, and slipped into the kitchen.

My brother sat back down on the couch, reaching for his guitar. I stood in the centre of the room, not knowing where to be.

'Jakey?'

'Yeah,' he murmured, looking down at his guitar.

'I've been writing stories.' I took a deep breath. 'Stories about us.'

He was quiet, holding his fingers on the strings but not making a sound.

'About what happened?' he asked finally.

'About everything.'

The silence stretched.

'It's not all inside me then,' I whispered. 'I can get it out.'

The truth of this seemed suddenly apparent.

'That's good,' he said slowly. 'It's good to get it out.'

He picked out a few notes on his guitar. I tried to listen to what they said. Sadness? Relief? Anxiety? It wasn't a language I quite understood.

'You going to write about this?' he asked, looking up at my face. 'About what I said?'

I stood there thinking about that. If it was my story to tell.

'Jakey, I don't know what's mine or yours.' I could feel my voice quivering. 'Maybe I never have.'

The kettle was boiling. I heard Gemma arranging the cups on the bench.

'Write it.' Jake plucked at the strings of his guitar, the sound soft, soothing. 'I want you to.'

'Will you read it?'

'I'll read all of it.'

I thought of the writing I'd already done, of what it would be like for my brother to read.

'It might be hard going.'

'It's better,' he said, 'than us carrying it around by ourselves.'

Gemma came in from the kitchen with the steaming teas. She put them down on the coffee table between us, sliding in beside my brother, smoothing a gentle hand down his arm. I watched her tender ministrations and a yearning broke open deep inside me. Still hovering, I wondered again where I should sit. It felt odd that after all these years I still couldn't find a way to be with them. I walked to the bookshelves and pulled out a book.

'Maybe I should read *Possession*?' I said, tucking the random book back in.

'Yeah?'

'I'm going to go look for it.'

≈

That night, ready for bed, I approached my mother in her island bedroom. Putting away her clothes, she was distracted.

'Mum?'

'Mmm?'

'I talked to Jake. About when Dad died.'

Startled, she turned to me in the doorway.

'What did he say?' She laid down a handful of long skirts on the bed.

'He told me about the day before Dad died. About how he told Dad that no one cared.'

'What?'

'He said that Dad was being intense and he told Dad that no one cared.'

She gazed past me, out through the door.

'I don't remember that,' she murmured. 'I don't remember that at all.'

'Jake said you knew he was really upset about it. You knew and rang Dad to make sure he was okay.'

I watched her face, wary of causing her grief.

'All I remember is that at some stage during that day I'd said to your father, "I'm ready to move on with my life." I know I said it at some point, just in passing. And when he wouldn't answer the phone the next day, I knew that he had done it, and I knew it was because of my words. That's all I remember about the day before he died.'

'Your words?'

'Yes …' She nodded. 'I mean, he was so close to the edge all the time, you remember?'

'What about Jake's words?'

My mother tucked her long hair behind her ear, and the familiar crease appeared on her brow.

'I don't know, Jess. I called your father most nights, to see if he was okay, or he called me. But all I remember is what I said. My words.'

We all have our own sentence, I thought. *Our own guilty words.*

I stood there, half inside the door, suspended at the edge of my mother's room.

'Mum?'

'Yeah?'

'How do we get rid of those words? How did you?'

She slowly shook her head. 'I don't think we can. It's just, after a while the words don't feel quite so heavy.'

'You learn to live with it?'

'They don't hold so much weight.'

'You can't float them out to sea?'

'Mmm…' Smiling at the thought, my mother turned from me and began to hang her skirts back on the rack. I thought of the photos I'd taken of my father's letter. How I'd wanted to let it go, but couldn't quite do it.

'Jess?'

'Yeah?'

'You okay?'

I glanced at the slates that covered the floor of my mother's bedroom, at the nozzle of the vacuum poking from beneath her bed.

'Yeah, I'm fine.'

'You sound a little sad.'

'No, I'm okay.'

I turned to look at the rack of my mother's clothes hung up against the wall and thought of the comfort of her long, flowing skirts. When I was small, my mother's gaze was a constant presence. I had talked and played and laughed beneath her sun-gaze, but sometimes—overwhelmed by the surveillance—I had searched around for shade. Curling myself against my mother's welcoming frame, I had hidden my face beneath her skirts, nuzzling in the shadowed darkness against her warm skin. Now, in her bedroom, I reached out a hand and traced the edge of the silk scarf that hung down beside the door.

'Mum?' I turned back towards her.

'Yeah?'

'I'm going to get up early and take the boys to the beach, to see the sunrise.'

My mother nodded, watching my face.

The chirping of crickets was loud in my ears. That tree, that birdsong, that rock, the feel of the slate beneath my feet, the very same bed where I had first felt my father's heartbeat banging beneath my tiny ear. I thought of my mother's strength, of her resilience. How it wasn't set like stone inside her, but something she chose anew each day. I stood a moment in her gaze, taking it

245

all in—this place, the site of my wounding but also my refuge—
then I turned and walked out the door.

≈

Staying in the one place, my memories had become overlaid,
one on top of the other, as though every new day had imprinted
its shape on me and I could no longer see what was underneath.
Instead, I remembered the textures of the past. The feel of the
bricks beneath my feet, the clacking sound of my rollerskates, the
smell of the rain in summer, the soft swish of my mother's skirts.

The forest itself was thick. It wasn't ornamental, like most
gardens, but vigorous and self-maintaining. The birdsong was
various and ever-present. Staghorns and elkhorns and mosses
and lichen grew on the tree trunks, the bromeliads endlessly
reproduced. It had its own microclimate. My parents had planted
it, but it felt timeless—eternal. I knew they'd had a vision when
they began, but I don't think they could have imagined just how
big or beautiful or self-sufficient each tree they lovingly patted
soil around could grow. Planting trees is a commitment to a
far-off future. There's something deeply hopeful about it. When
I was a kid, growing in this growing forest, the future seemed
endlessly bright. Everything was wildly fertile, all around me
teeming with life.

When Zoe died my father had erected that giant log in the
garden in memory of her, planning to carve her name into it like
a tombstone, but—overcome by grief—he never did. Once a rich,

woody brown, the log was now shrunken and grey. Furrows ran down it in vertical lines—the rain had made its mark. It looked, quite simply, like a dead tree, where once it had all the majesty of a monument. When my father first erected the log, it was large and imposing, but the trees had grown around it, dwarfing it in size. My sister, her life cut so short. She stopped being, while the forest lived on. When my father thought to memorialise Zoe with this grand, half-finished gesture, he couldn't know how apt a symbol it would one day become. My sister's log. The dead still here among the living.

People often proclaim that what's needed is a fresh start, and I understood the allure. The temptation to begin again, to wipe the slate clean. But sometimes you had to stick around to see things come to fruition. Some trees live hundreds of years. The magnitude of those lifespans are hard for the human mind to comprehend. How can we know, when we plant those seeds, just how extraordinary the trees might become?

My home in the forest contained so many layers of memory it was difficult to experience them with any clarity. The hope and the loss and the joy and the sorrow, like seams of soil, building and building. There was a density to it, this layering of memory, a richness. I looked out my bedroom windows at the gentle sway of the moonlit leaves, the trees so solid, so enduring. *I was planted here*, I thought. *What will I become?*

≈

I suspect many of us have a shadow-walker, a damaged self too maimed to bring into the light. Each one of us is wounded in some way, carrying secret scars. Why is it that we are called upon to hide them? My father's grief was too large for the forest to hold, but what if there had been a space for him—out in the world—to inhabit that sorrow? A space without stigma or the threat of exclusion. And my sister too. What if Zoe hadn't been forced to live all those parallel lives? To pretend everything was fine when it obviously wasn't? Being in pain isn't a form of failure; it just means you're alive. It's time we stopped casting out those among us who are hurt or frightened. Those among us who have been harmed. A wound isn't contagious, but it's slow to heal if it receives no tending. We need to bring them back from the other side of the river, all those shadow-walkers. It is dark there, and they are dying in great numbers. Setting themselves on fire. One by one.

≈

Driving to the beach, my gaze darted between the road and my sleepy children snuggled up on the back seat. Awake but slouching, Milla stared out the window at the silhouetted trees. Luca's cheek sagged against his seatbelt, eyes closed in sleep, lips rosebud pink. A dull ache lingered behind my brow and I lifted my hand to push against my forehead, trying to press the pain away. Gradually lightening, the sky was opening before us, and Milla sat up, spine straight, to peer out the window.

As we pulled up at the headland, the horizon was tinged an impossible red. Milla and I clambered from the car.

'Mum, what's that?' Milla's eyes were disbelieving as he watched the sky.

'It's the sunrise, baby. The sun coming up, the night turning into day.'

'We better wake Luca up.' Milla's voice was low, serious. 'He won't want to miss this.'

I leaned back against the bonnet of the car. Milla trotted to Luca's window and pulled the door open. He unclicked his brother's seatbelt and tugged at Luca's limp hand.

'Luca, wake up and look at the sky.'

Tumbling from his seat, sleepy-eyed and clumsy, Luca lurched towards me. Squinting sideways at the slow rise of red from the horizon, he nudged against my side and I wrapped my arm around his small shoulder.

'It's a sunrise,' Milla stated, presenting the facts. 'When the sun comes over the horizon. Beginning of the morning.'

Face soft, eyes wide, Luca stared out at the ocean and the luminous colour. The red was melting into orange and pink, and moving upwards across the sky. The tip of the sun burned brightly at the edge of the skyline.

'Could I swim out there?' Milla asked, pointing out towards the sun.

'No, the horizon is just an illusion. You can't get to it, just like you can't reach up and touch the sky.' I lifted my free arm high above my head and wiggled my fingers.

'An illusion? Like a unicorn or a dragon?' Milla glanced up at my fingers, then back at my face.

'No, baby. Illusions are when what you see isn't exactly how things are. It looks like the sea meets the sky just out there, that the sun is coming up across a straight line—but really the earth is round like a ball, and there are no edges to reach, no straight lines. It's a trick of the eye. An illusion.'

'What are dragons and unicorns, then?'

'Stories that people tell. Myths.'

The waves rolled softly towards the shore, glimmering with fresh sunlight. Milla pulled his shirt over his head.

'What are you doing, gorgeous?' I asked.

'Going for a swim ...'

'Not yet—wait until it's properly light. Let's go down and sit on the sand.'

The feathery grass of the sand dune rustled in the breeze. Wandering downwards, I watched as Milla and Luca jumped from smudgy footprint to smudgy footprint, treading an ancient path to the shore. Crossing the beach, a crab flicked from hole to hole and I bent and touched the rolled spheres of sand that littered the tiny burrows. Milla stopped and poked his finger inside a round opening.

'Do you think I can catch one, Mum?'

'You'll have to be fast.'

The sun was a half-circle on the horizon, the sky suddenly bright, colour seeping up into the blue. Milla and Luca ran to the edge of the water, but I drifted above the waterline to the place where I'd made the fisherman's silhouette. Shells and rocks were strewn about, evidence of a weathered construction, but the print of the man was gone. I thought of Sam and felt my heartbeat quicken. Excitement or fear, it was hard to tell. I wondered if I could uncross my wires. I knew I would try, my willingness a new brightness opening up inside me. One step at a time.

Looking along the dunes, there were dry-tossed branches tangled in bunches of dune grass, and I moved forward to pull them free. Selecting two pieces of grey driftwood, I poked the branches in the sand next to the mess of shells. I drew a circle around the upright wood, and watched my creation as it was slowly lit up by the sun.

The children's voices carried across the sand, and I turned to see them jumping the sliding veil of the shallow waves, pale bodies shining with stray drops of water, the sun a yellow ball against the sky. At the shore, the hard sand around my feet was patterned in furrowed, stretching arms. The children's pyjamas lay sprawled on the dry sand above, abandoned. I watched as a spiralling wave collapsed inwards and glided towards the shore, rushing in a final surge across my toes. The water was cool and I looked down at the clear, bubbling wave.

Breaking the silence in my family felt monumental. We had shielded each other from our pain, but the price of that had been loneliness. I didn't want to be quiet anymore and I didn't want to be alone. Not trusting anyone, not trusting myself. All those years I'd been afraid, as though inside me a wildness prowled that might one day burst the banks. But I had been steady. The storms

I had weathered and still kept my feet. That life force my father had given me—his intensity, his passion, his impulsivity, his fearlessness, his creativity, his drive—I wanted it all back. That wild bright light and all its potential.

Stepping back from the water, I pulled off my clothes.

'Mum, what are you doing?' Milla stopped jumping and looked at me, head cocked to the side.

'I'm coming in, boys. I'm coming in.'

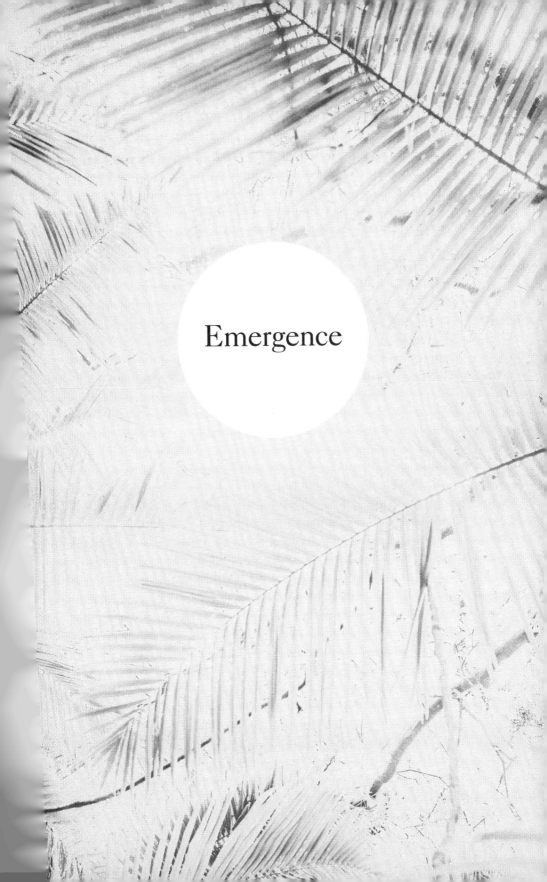

Emergence

A narrative is a powerful thing, laying down a road that can be walked, a path that can be seen behind you. You can look back and witness how far you've come. Writing—that simple act of arranging words in a line—allowed me to bring order to parts of my life that had seemed deeply chaotic. Before I found a way to sense-make through words, I felt tossed about like a leaf caught in rough surf, unable to get to shore.

Through writing, I discovered a language that made telling my story possible. I believed once I'd finished that would be it. I'd have gotten the whole lot off my chest, and there'd be no more left to say. But as I moved from my twenties into my thirties, I faced a whole new set of experiences, as everyone does. New relationships, new heartbreaks. To my surprise, I kept on writing. Invented stories, told in another person's voice, based around incidents and encounters that had never occurred. I began to write fiction in an attempt to understand the new complexities of my world. In the years that followed I wrote two novels, back to back, and in an improbable series of events they were published.

Being published required my participation in realms outside the forest of my childhood. Stepping into the world after such a long period of seclusion was stepping into the unknown. In my home in the forest we had no mobile phone reception, limited fuzzy television and only dial-up internet, which I had never really used. I didn't know about online communities or blogging. I'd never been to a writers' festival. These things were beyond the periphery of my small world. All that time I'd been wondering about my tribe—whether or not it even existed—and there you all were.

For me, emerging from grief hasn't been about leaving home, moving on, or even letting go. It hasn't been about hiking a mountain trail or travelling the world or starting life again in a more exotic place. It's been about sharing words—slowly, tentatively—sharing words with you.

In truth, I wish that my dead ones were here to tell their own stories. That I wasn't left—the unofficial archivist—sorting through the clues. The search for truth is rife with complexity, littered with unknowable possibilities. Maybe all we can ever do is acknowledge and bear witness to one another's stories.

≈

At its heart, grief entails learning to live with the consequences of love. Without love, there is no grief, for nothing has been lost. Connection, intimacy, affection, attachment. For me, these things have come to seem delicate, fragile even. Knowing this,

256

I try to treat them tenderly. But living in the forest almost all of my life, cohabiting with my adolescent trauma, I've come to see the inevitability of uncertainty. Even in the forest I can't keep it at bay.

These days, I'm not so wary, not so stiff and sore. The line between destruction and perfection no longer feels quite so fine. Sometimes I'll still cry when I hear the word 'trust'. Certain things, once broken, are hard to mend, and often the least visible scars last the longest. But deep down, I know that I've been lucky, that not everyone is born into a sea of green, or could possibly live in the place of their wounding and find it healing or transforming. Home has been my balm, my consolation.

Stillness—a kind of moving. Staying—a kind of grace.

Acknowledgments

I would like to acknowledge the support of the Australia Council of the Arts in the creation of this work. Big thanks also to Varuna, The Writers' House, where I spent two separate fellowships working on this project, many years apart.

To the early readers of this memoir—Varda Shepherd, Sarah Armstrong, Neil Buhrich, Lhasa Morgan, Peter Bishop, Donica Bettanin, James Murray, Anna Sabadini—I still remember all your words of encouragement. Thank you for being so gentle with me.

Special recognition for my agent, Jenny Darling, who fought tooth and nail to get the text up to scratch. I could not have done it without you. Also to Mary Rennie, who championed this work so fiercely from the outset.

Thanks always to those beautiful shiny-shiny girls—Louise Nicholls, Danika Cottrell, Rose Anderson, Ruby Rozental and Rachel Scarrabelotti. I'll never forget your kindness. And to Niki Huang, Laura Rosen, Jane Osborne, Jahnavi Vinden-Clark, Olivia Ross-Wilson, Gemma Holston, Gabriel Finardi, Bradley McCann, Matt Hagan, Crissy Tomarelli, Michael Elliot, Marlene Farry, Emma Kearney, Romy Ash, Sean Anderson, Anna Krien, Tracy Farr, Eliza Henry Jones, Hayley Katzen, Jane Rawson, Penny Nelson, Joseph Bell, Josephine Browne, Lilli Waters, Amanda Patterson, Siboney, Lisa Walker, Jane Camens, Helen Burns and Michelle Taylor for friendship, inspiration and support. Thanks also to my beau, who—tentatively—has showed me a new kind of care.

Many thanks to Elizabeth Cowell and the whole team at Text, who have demonstrated such enormous sensitivity and commitment throughout the process of bringing this work to publication.

To my remaining siblings, Billie and Jacob, my mother, Jan Smith, and my sons, Milla and Luca—a special thanks. Without each of you—and your monumental love and generosity—there would be no *Staying*.

Finally, to my dead ones—Zoe Matilda Cole and Ian Gordon Cole. The brightest of falling stars. I still miss you.